Another Country

Real Life Beyond Rose Cottage

James Garo Derounian

NCVO Publications

Published by
NCVO Publications
(incorporating Bedford Square Press)
imprint of the
National Council for
Voluntary Organisations

Regent's Wharf
8 All Saints Street
London N1 9RL

First published 1993
© NCVO 1993

Typeset by GCS, Leighton Buzzard, Beds.
Printed in Great Britain by Staples
Printers Rochester Limited

A catalogue record for this book is
available from the British Library.

ISBN 0 7199 1395 0

Dedication

To Linsey, who heard a lot about 'the state of England's countryside' in 1992, with much love.
Also for Dad, John, Zabelle, Aunty Haines, Samuel and Flora, who provide so much support and encouragement.

Contents

List of Figures

Foreword

Life in the English countryside has undergone massive changes this century. The growth in personal mobility brought about by the advent of the motor car and by increased personal affluence has opened up the countryside to millions of people. We now have a new breed of country dwellers and as recent surveys have shown many others aspire to a rural lifestyle as an escape from city life.

Traditional employment patterns have changed also. If you work in a rural area you are now more likely to be engaged in a service industry or in manufacturing than in farming or mining. Modern technology has widened the locational options for many businesses and enabled entrepreneurs and managers to give more weight to their desire to establish their businesses in a pleasant environment.

In many parts of England the countryside is thriving: population is increasing, self-employment and new business formation is growing, registered unemployment is widely below the national average. But appearances can deceive: the picturesque rose has its thorns. Rural England, and more importantly the people there, face a number of growing problems – lack of jobs in some areas, high house prices, declining services and pressures against development from those who believe that protecting the environment means preserving it as it is.

The Rural Development Commission believes that the best way to conserve the countryside is through the maintenance of a healthy rural economy and communities with people from all walks of life and in a range of circumstances. We do not want the countryside to be available only to the able, mobile and better-off members of our society.

We cannot and would not want to stem the economic and social changes which are occurring in the countryside but we can help to bring about a better understanding on the part of newcomers and urban residents about the problems and needs facing some rural dwellers, especially the less well-off and the less mobile.

This book illustrates some of those problems and will, I hope, help to dispel some of the myths surrounding life in the countryside. It contains some messages for all of us. For those who operate, or seek to influence, the planning system it demonstrates that rural areas must be allowed to adapt to changing circumstances. For those with responsibility for policies, programmes and services the message is that these may have a different impact in rural areas. Policies may need to be adapted and delivery systems to be flexible. For all of us – in the private, public and voluntary sectors – it underlines the case for viewing the countryside in the round and collaborating on finding a balance between economic, social and environmental aspirations which respects the needs of everyone in rural communities.

I hope this book will further the growing interest in and understanding of rural issues.

Richard Butt
Chief Executive, Rural Development Commission

Preface

*Refer to 'social problems' and the politicians and public have a mental
image of the inner city. Refer to 'rural problems' and the image is
one of conservation, agriculture and the environment.*
Malcolm Moseley, Director of ACRE,
England's Rural Communities Charity, September 1992

Another Country explores aspects of rural life that are rarely
acknowledged: crime, disadvantage, black people in villages,
homelessness. There is no attempt to cover every facet of country
living – farming or rural transport, for example, are barely
mentioned. This is an introduction to an alternative vision of rural
England – one which recognises strengths and weaknesses.

The trouble is that if people think about the countryside at all,
they remember it fondly. The image-makers have been hard at work
conspiring to protect, conserve and sanitise the way we look at
country life. Even the word 'country' conjures images, not just of
rustic charm – 'country cottages', 'country produce' – but also of
nationhood. A central difficulty is that rural areas are venerated and
felt to enshrine the nation's spirit and soul.

I was born during 1957 and brought up in north London, a few
miles from Broadwater Farm where rioting took place in the 1980s
and a short way from the Kray twins' stamping ground of Finsbury
Park. Greenery was in short supply. Between school and university I
worked as a community service volunteer (CSV) alongside Haringey
social workers. My tasks were varied – minding autistic children,

visiting mentally ill people in the community and checking that modifications had been carried out in accordance with occupational therapists' instructions. Haringey taught me a lot about the dreadful conditions in which many vulnerable citizens live – the old, the sick and the poor. But it came as quite a shock to find these same groups struggling and silent, buried deep beneath a facade of rural well-being.

At Wye Agricultural College in Kent I had the chance to look at the countryside from an environmental, social and economic standpoint. What became clear was that the land and landscape *are* the people. John Gummer, the Minister for Agriculture in 1992, recounts an apocryphal story about a new priest walking the lanes of his parish. He stops to converse with one of his flock – a farmer, 'Isn't it marvellous what God and mankind can achieve together?' The old boy fixes the young cleric and replies, 'Yes – but you should have seen it when the Lord had it all to Himself!'

My university education also introduced the idea of conflicting interests at work in the countryside. Professor Gerald Wibberley likened the country to a giant 'green jelly' at a party. Some people want to 'conserve' it; others would like to 'consume' it. The march of time has seen the agricultural lobby in retreat, suffering a barrage of defeats centring on the ripping up of hedgerows, salmonella in eggs, fertiliser run-off into watercourses and the subsidised over-supply of milk and other produce that no one wants to buy. Furthermore, Gerald Wibberley gave sound advice about job hunting: 'If you think that you'll walk out with a degree and straight into the job of your dreams, you have a nasty shock ahead of you. Your working life, if you are fortunate, is a gradual progression towards what best suits you.' My own 'gradual progression' has taken in farmwork, rural research, a countryside officer post in Devon, rural development work in Northumberland and lecturing in planning at the University of Newcastle.

Experience to date has reinforced my belief that the future of the English countryside lies in effectively harnessing the energy of local people, so that they can direct and influence their own destinies. It is also true that an assumed affluence among villagers hides significant problems of low pay, poverty, homelessness, mental illness and suicide, to name but a few.

The English countryside concerns us all – as residents or visitors, farmers or consumers. Town and country need each other. And each requires active concern from local people as well as by those outsiders that set the policies and dictate the parameters of everyday life.

Another Country goes beyond the advertising slogans and cherished 'rural values'. The combination of hard fact and personal testimony may shock the reader. In the end this book is meant to be a 'good read', an engaging one and a searchlight on an overgrown corner of our national identity. It is a call to arms for policy-makers, funding agencies – voluntary and statutory organisations of all kinds – and concerned individuals.

James Derounian

Acknowledgements

This book was produced with the help of the Rural Development Commission, the UK Branch of the Calouste Gulbenkian Foundation and the BT Community Programme. Ben Whitaker at the Calouste Gulbenkian Foundation had the initial idea for a work along the lines of *Another Country*.

If there is a competition for 'best secretary in the UK', Susan Middleton has to be the winner.

Sally Lawson helped in researching the section on mental illness. Dr Allan Peggie of the Northumbria Probation Service, and Chair of the National Probation Research and Information Exchange, provided invaluable material on rural crime. I am very grateful to both.

Jeremy Fennell and colleagues at ACRE have been unstintingly helpful and generous with their time. The *Rural Digest* was a constant source of reference.

Sarah Buchanan and Jackie Sallon at NCVO provided useful editorial input.

David Clark has helped me, on a range of issues, over many years.

My thanks to Michaela Dungate, Gayle Kirrage, Neil Shenton and 'Community Contact', for original research into rural deprivation and the response of voluntary organisations.

The following have helped in various ways: staff at Rural Community Councils (RCCs)/ACRE branches in Bedfordshire, Derbyshire, Devon, Hampshire, Hertfordshire, Lincolnshire, Norfolk, Northumberland, Shropshire, Somerset, Suffolk, Sussex and Wiltshire. Also Julian Agyeman, Robert Arckless, Barbara

Browne, Don Bates, Alan Baty, BBC Radio 4, Rachel Billings, Eleanor Button, John Clark, Paul Cloke, Angie Corby, Bengt Dahlgren, Sarah Day, John Derounian, Helen Dimond, Sheila Dixon, Pat Dolan, Michael Dower, Beatriz Drury, Ann Dunlop, David Elliott, Carmel Fox, Marion Guiry, Monica Haigh, Joyce Halliday, Deborah Hamilton, Mike Hamp, Noel Hardy, Alison Holden, David Hughes, Stephen Hugh-Jones, Eric Jay, Fr Jim, Bernard Lane, Greg Lawrence, Sarah Lawrenson, Alison Locke, Brian McLaughlin, Pat McMullen, Paul Mardell, Alison Marshall, Baroness Masham, Jennie Merriman, David Miller, Mintel International, 'Mr Mistry', Crispin Moor, Peter Newell, Elaine Oldham, Sandra Oliver, Robin Osmond, Daniel Pearson, David Rabson, Karen Richardson, Liz Rodrigo, Alan Rogers, Mustafa Shaikh, Jan Sherlock, Posy Simmonds, David Smith, Moira Stone, Di Stubbs, Chris Taylor, Kirsty White, Peter White, Gerald Wibberley, Steve Wilcox, Mike Winter, Women's Farm and Garden Association, Noelle Wright, Carol Young.

Thank you all.

Part one

Setting the scene

Chapter 1

A Green and Pleasant Land?

Why bother with the countryside? Not many of us live there, and most villagers are well-heeled anyway. It's tempting to agree with this view and just leave well enough alone. This after all has been the approach of successive governments. But is the country really such a haven of stability and prosperity?

Ten million people, one-fifth of the population, live and work in rural England. In land-use terms the country assumes even greater significance: at least two-thirds of England and Wales can be said to be 'rural'. And the view through the car windscreen confirms this – rolling hills, open fields, villages and market towns. But for modern Man – *Homo Urbanicus* – the countryside tends to be seen as a theatrical backcloth to city life. A place of rest for the commuter, somewhere to visit on holiday or at weekends. These images are valid in their own right, but only scratch the surface of what it is like, for many, to live in England's countryside.

Any idea of the rural idyll lasts 30 seconds when you visit these places.

Lord Shuttleworth speaking about some
coalfield communities, 1992

Four giant chimneystacks pierce the sky. An overhead gantry straddles the main road. Mounds of coal lower on the horizon. Brick-built miners' houses and allotments lie in the shadow of two power stations: all concrete and corrugated, one of these is in the process of being decommissioned. Freight trains carry aluminium ore to a nearby smelter. The river with its rotting harbour on one side, the dunes and North Sea on the other. There's a stink of fish oil and the constant movement of men in white overalls – ear defenders up on their crash hats like mutant versions of Mickey Mouse. Whole streets have been torn down and blue asbestos leaks into the poisoned earth. Wasteland, tipper trucks, split-bridges, grabbing machines, cranes and dockland punctuate the scene. Until very recently the rusted and scoured conning-tower of a Russian submarine reared its head from a breaker's yard. 666 – the 'number of the beast' – stood out from the rusted shell. Now the site lies empty. The corner shop is partly boarded and the church shuttered for protection. These images don't come from the inner-city, but they are taken from life.

Welcome to the tiny communities of Cambois and North Blyth on England's east coast. Reverend Jim Smith describes them as 'close-knit, working class villages. Cambois originally housed coal families and North Blyth was made up of railwaymen.' 'Jimmy' Smith, a pit electrician for 42 years, is now the non-stipendary priest serving these communities.

At one time people were left to 'God and good neighbours'. Then the local council shattered the calm. On the plus side, people have begun to realise that they can influence decisions made by outside authorities. I take an essentially optimistic view of life: when I arrived in 1988 St Andrew's Church was half empty on a Sunday, now it's half full!

Villages are often portrayed as tranquil places. Imagine, then, how the residents of North Blyth felt when they first saw local authority plans for their area up to the year 2000: 'Wansbeck District Council will require and demolish all 86 dwellings at Worsdell Street, Dale Street and Gray Street, North Blyth, to facilitate the development of port-related industry.' Those '86 dwellings' meant that an entire hamlet was to be wiped out. After a hard fight the District has scrapped its planned demolition work. That success, in addition to others such as the establishment of a branch surgery in the old Miners' Welfare, has meant that some measure of independence has been regained. And there are a few other hopeful signs: the first school has a healthy roll of 65 pupils; St Andrew's Church is now as neat and clean as a new pin. The interior and memorial garden bear witness to the commitment of the 20 or so regular church-goers. The community has begun to question decisions rather than to accept the outcome.

Cambois, like many rural communities, is in a state of painful transition. Father Jim points to the old RC church, built for the Irish workers who constructed the power station, but 'now turned into a storehouse; the chapel is boarded up – it has by turns been a cinema and boys' club – today it stands as another relic to a bygone era; the power station is laying off several hundred men and the ship-breakers lies silent. Cambois hardly inspires hope for the future.

This is a landscape of extremes, dominated by the power stations, which look like a cross between Battersea and Chernobyl. 'Sickly sweet smells come over from the pharmaceutical plant producing penicillin; acrid fish oil mixes in from another direction; white ash from the freight terminal periodically escapes', complains Father Jim. And he concludes by saying that 'the greater poverty that pervades the area comes from the loss of a large part of the community that once was Cambois and the spirit that went with them.'

The message from Cambois and North Blyth is challenging and direct: rural communities are not automatically well-to-do, pretty places. Some are highly industrial and suffer all the attendant problems of a degraded environment. Figure 1 shows how rural and urban communities shared many difficulties in 1980. In 1993 the overlap, as this book shows, is much greater.

I fear too much of the truth would prove painful to our listeners.

Liz Rigbey, former producer of The Archers, 1986

The myth of a rural idyll can be laid firmly at the door of the image-makers – certain politicians, the media and many engaged in the arts. Advertising has also exercised a pernicious influence. For

North Blyth Community with Blyth Power Station behind
(Duncan Davis)

example, a 1991 British Rail poster reads: 'English landscape art. A private view. In first class... enjoy the fact that you have the best private seat for one of the best shows on earth; the English countryside.' This contains a series of misleading impressions – the country as an unchanging masterpiece, an open air playground and the idea of privilege with one important grain of truth: the countryside, like a work of art, is the product of human endeavour. And this is the first reason why we should bother about rural England. What we do, or neglect to do, does make a difference. A countryside stripped of people, with villages decaying and land reverting to the wild is not a pretty view – even from a car or train. But rural decline is not a new concept. In 1762 Oliver Goldsmith wrote about 'The Deserted Village', and observed that 'wherever the traveller turns, while he sees one part of the inhabitants of the country becoming immensely rich, he sees the other growing miserably poor'.

Figure I Urban and rural Britain – overlapping sets of problems

Inner Urban	Outer Rural	Overlapping Problems
Physical environment	*Inaccessibility*	*Economic stagnation*
Derelict land	● to services and jobs	Declining demand for
Blighted land	*High per capita costs*	labour
Visual/noise pollution	of services (public	● high unemployment
Racial tension	and private)	● low wages
Social pathology	*High percentage of*	● wrong skills
● delinquency	*elderly people*	● poor job
● drug addiction etc.	● effects on society	opportunities for
Problems from	● costs of servicing	school leavers
overcrowding/high		*Population decline*
density		● loss of dynamic
		elements
		● *Decline of services*
		(public & private)
		Little new investment
		(public or private)
		Gentrification/second
		homes
		Declining morale and
		community spirit
		Housing markets
		which 'lock in' the
		poor

Source: Malcolm Moseley, 'Is rural deprivation really rural?', *The Planner*, July 1980

One of the greatest obstacles to understanding rural society is the word 'country'. It encompasses nationhood, a sense of belonging and at the same time refers to the open spaces beyond the cities. You can almost hear the buzz of a bee on a still and bright summer's day, long ago in childhood. The fatal attraction of rural England is deeply embedded in our national subconscious. From Beatrix Potter's lakeland illustrations to Winnie the Pooh in the Ashdown Forest and Little Grey Rabbit whose activities 'were the country ways known to the author'. But Alison Uttley also observed the dark nights that 'were detested by the farm hands, the wind was like a carving knife and it cut their hands and cheeks until they bled'. This is a side of rural life which has been discreetly veiled.

The countryside has attracted veneration, but there is a strong undercurrent which has highlighted ignorance, corruption and claustrophobia. Thomas Hardy talks of villages 'full of strife and noise, old senseless gossips and blackguarding boys'. So the country has never been, except in imagination, a Garden of Eden. The same ambivalence is also true in relation to city life. Many have viewed the city as a place of learning, progress and dynamism. But equally William Wordsworth described 'The close and overcrowded haunts of cities, where the human heart is sick', the endless stream of people, 'the deafening din'. Rural and urban areas share many qualities; problems are not exclusive to the city nor is quality of life guaranteed in the country.

> ... There is almost an inverse proportion, in the twentieth century, between the relative importance of the working rural economy and the cultural importance of rural ideas.
>
> *Raymond Williams, 1975*

As the population has shifted from a rural to a predominantly urban existence, so the beatification of the countryside has become increasingly pronounced. The playwright J.B. Priestley, writing in the 1930s, argued for preservation: 'Before the mines and factories came, and long before we went from bad to worse with our arterial roads and petrol stations and horrible brick bungalows, this country must have been an enchantment, designed by God to be the earthly paradise of wandering water-colourists.' People's need for jobs and housing are forgotten when we are presented with an idyllic view of the eighteenth century, a time when landlords were not averse to evicting tenants and flattening their homes to make way for a carefully re-created landscape. It's a sort of 3-D painting minus humans.

The latter part of the twentieth century has witnessed the growth of interest/pressure groups peddling preservation. The National Trust slogan, 'I'm one in a million', is no idle boast and their membership currently exceeds 2.5 million. Then there is the RSPB (Royal Society for the Protection of Birds) which conserves bird habitats and species 'either by owning and managing land itself or by influencing land-use practices'. It has just under 1 million members, an income of more than £22 million and controls 118 nature reserves covering 180,500 acres, quite significant for a voluntary organisation.

As the government's Countryside Commission pointed out in 1987, 'If the livelihood of rural people is undermined, the countryside itself will become less attractive... so it is in the national interest, and not simply in the rural interest, that there should continue to be a thriving countryside.' Lord Vinson, a landowner and past chairman of another agency – the Rural Development Commission (RDC) – reinforced this point.

> We must not allow two visions of the countryside to develop: the green and pleasant land which people visit and fantasise about, and the place where many people live and work and which has to pay for its upkeep... the interdependence of countryside conservation and the promotion of its economic and social welfare is being overlooked. They need each other.

The idea of economic development and conservation going hand in hand provides a further reason why we should bother about rural England. Here is an ideal opportunity to protect our heritage by putting it to productive use. There is a tendency to forget that many industrial ruins would, in their heyday, have been noisy, smelly and unsightly blots on the landscape. The Cornish tin and Durham lead mines are as much a fact of rural history as the legacy of past farming techniques.

Coalfield Communities

Farmed land is perceived as the 'real countryside'. In reality rural communities come in all shapes and forms. There are coastal villages with the remains of a fishing industry, increasingly dependent on poorly paid and seasonal tourism. Some Devon and Cornish seaside communities are obvious examples.

And further still from the traditional view of the village are rural coalfield communities. In the East Midlands and South Yorkshire, for example, pit closures have added 30,000 people to the dole queue since 1984. Wholesale closure of deep mines, announced in October 1992, with 10,000 jobs to be lost in rural communities will only

At Clipstone in Nottinghamshire, the feeling is that the closures will devastate the area
(Trevor Clayton)

compound the problem. These places are 'betwixt and between'– neither inner city nor remote rural areas. They face their own peculiar problems of environmental decay, poor housing, loss of community confidence and leadership. Fletchertown in West Cumbria is typical of many mining villages with its rows of small terraced houses built on a grid pattern. Eric Nixon, a local councillor, recalls that

> the late 1960s and early 1970s witnessed a substantial decline in community life... previously strong village institutions such as the sports clubs and social activities withered or disappeared; the Parish Council became less active and concerned only with immediate issues.... Perhaps the most telling sign was the fact that by the late 1980s a village of about 200 dwellings and over 400 people could only produce 8–10 children for the school.

The 'Lake District' may be on its doorstep but for good looks, Fletchertown might as well be on another planet.

Shadows, Ghosts and 'Planned' Villages

'Shadow' communities are those which feel the gravitational pull of a nearby city. These can experience acute problems of exorbitant house prices, unbalanced communities resulting from a preponderance of commuters and restrictive 'green belt' planning policies inhibiting new developments which are the lifeblood of any village. The Bedfordshire settlement of Sundon lies about three miles north of Luton. In a local opinion poll the population of around 600 was split down the middle – half wanted the place to remain as a village with a distinct identity, while the other 50 per cent were happy to see themselves become a suburb of Luton. Alison Locke at the Bedfordshire Rural Community Council (RCC) cites another example, where new development has got out of hand. Elstow village with around 800 population is about to double in size and coalesce with nearby Bedford. Plans for the construction of 400 houses have been approved.

'Ghost' villages are found in remote and beautiful corners of our island. The eleven National Parks in England and Wales – created because of their outstanding natural beauty – also harbour some of the worst examples of these part-time villages, bustling in the summer but virtually derelict for much of the year. Some settlements in south Devon, for example, have more than one in four of their houses as holiday or second homes.

Exford is a small community on Exmoor. During the 1980s its Parish Council estimated that one-third of the entire housing stock was not permanently occupied. David Smith, a rural community worker in Somerset, has no doubt that such a high proportion of 'occasional' properties has 'polarised the village between holiday and second-home owners, on the one hand, and those who live in Exford throughout the year, on the other'. David Rabson, from the Exmoor National Park Authority, points to 'a widespread need in terms of affordable housing for local people to rent or purchase. The relocation of significant numbers of people from outside the area, to holiday homes or for retirement, is undoubtedly increasing the pressure on our villages.'

There are also 'planned' communities. These are places built and largely owned by a single landowner. Many estate villages are hundreds of years old. 'Forestry' villages, by contrast, are a twentieth-century phenomenon. Byrness, Kielder and Stonehaugh, near the Scottish border, were created by the Forestry Commission to house its employees. Longhoughton on the northeastern seaboard experiences a rather different form of institutional influence – it has its own NAAFI and acts as a dormitory for RAF Boulmer. The end of the 'Cold War' and expected peace dividend are calling into question the dependence of some areas on military establishments.

In 1989 researchers at the University of East Anglia estimated that closure of the United States Air Force bases at Woodbridge and Bentwaters, northeast of Ipswich, would have a disastrous effect on local firms. Roughly 7,000 annual contracts exist between the bases and companies located within a 25-mile radius. The Rural Development Commission believes that the rural areas of Suffolk,

North Yorkshire, Lincolnshire, Devon and Wiltshire stand to be particularly hard hit by the rundown of UK personnel.

The 1991 Census confirms that people are moving from the cities back into the country. This may, in part, reflect another ideal – elevating a house in the country near the top of the list of social aspirations. Holiday and childhood memories can cloud the reality of making a new start in an alien setting, living at a distance from hospitals and other services previously taken for granted.

New Villagers

Newcomers to a village are often portrayed as 'outsiders', who threaten to change the character of a community and its institutions. In the case of 'ghost' villages such fears may well be founded. And yet settlements can and must change if they are to adapt and flourish. A transfusion of new blood is a delicate operation for any village and must not be allowed to induce a haemorrhage of younger, local people, forced out by relatively rich new arrivals. There needs to be a willingness to participate on the part of a 'new' villager, tempered by a sensitivity to the established ways of doing things. Equally, longer-standing residents should welcome those who have only recently arrived, while actively preserving and articulating local distinctiveness. Anthony Russell, who advised the Archibishops' 1991 Commission on Rural Areas, offers a cogent explanation for the potential conflict between 'old' and 'new' villagers: the former belong to a place 'in the sense of being totally identified in both family and work with a particular settlement'. Belonging is a matter of identification, absorbing the essence of a place through some form of historical osmosis.

> By contrast, the new villagers tend to understand the phrase 'belonging to the village' in terms of participation. For them it is important to be involved in and committed to organisations and activities which take place within the village; that is the only way, in their terms, of demonstrating both to the village and to themselves that they belong to this particular

settlement. They tend to be critical both of those old villagers who seem, in their eyes, 'not to care about what goes on in the village', and of those new villagers who take no part in village activities.

But it would be totally false to assume that the only likely split is between established and more recent residents. Much older are periodic clashes between church and chapel, landlord and labourer, master and servant, owner and tenant. The current wave of urban–rural migration has been blamed wrongly for usurping and despoiling a previously idyllic rural society. Joseph Arch was a founder of the National Agricultural Labourers Union in 1872. He described an early meeting:

> I mounted an old pig-stool, and in the flickering light of the lanterns I saw the earnest upturned faces of these poor brothers of mine – faces gaunt with hunger and pinched with want. These white slaves of England stood there with the darkness all about them, like the Children of Israel waiting for someone to lead them out of the land of Egypt.

Nowadays the agricultural workforce is a dying breed for different reasons. Rising productivity based on mechanisation has meant that between 1978 and 1988 the total numbers engaged in UK agriculture fell from 758,000 to 664,000, a loss of 94,000 (12 per cent). The Rural Development Commission gauges 'that there will be a larger loss of full-time jobs (farmers and employees) from farming in the present decade than was experienced in the last decade, perhaps as high as 100,000 or more'. And the Agricultural Training Board predicts a consequent loss of jobs dependent on farming, in the order of 55,000 between 1990 and 1995. Lord Shuttleworth, the RDC's Chairman, sees a hard road ahead. 'As farming requires both less people and less land, a range of issues emerges: replacing jobs, new uses for land, the quality of life for rural dwellers, protecting the quality of the rural environment in the interests of all the population of England.' The city and the country are inextricably bound together. A healthy and productive countryside serves to benefit the nation as a whole.

This introduction has drawn back the lace curtain at 'Rose Cottage', so that the clouds as well as the glories of rural England can be glimpsed. Succeeding chapters will fill in the picture. The next chapter shows how powerfully myths about the countryside have deformed policy-making. Chapters 3, 4 and 5 look at what it is like to be disadvantaged in this 'green and pleasant land'. Equally important, the ways in which individuals, villages, the public and private sectors are tackling such issues, will be highlighted (Chapter 6). The concluding chapter offers a vision for the future and encourages readers to explore their own potential for forging 'Another Country'.

Chapter 2

Policy and Practice – The Impact of Myths

The Thin Trickle of Rural Resources

It wouldn't matter if misconceptions about the countryside had no practical effect. But they do. A popular impression that rural England is entirely agricultural and peopled by farmers dramatically illustrates the point.

The National Economic Development Office (NEDO) calculated that the total number of people engaged in UK agriculture was 664,000 in 1988. 'Although the proportion of waged employment accounted for by agriculture is only 1.5 per cent for England, it is around 10 per cent for rural areas in general,' observes the Rural Development Commission. So if one-tenth of the English rural workforce is employed in agriculture, does this mean that one-tenth of government resources benefit the farmer? Definitely not.

Researchers at Wye Agricultural College concluded in 1989 that 'among the intended beneficiaries, farmers were clearly the main group as measured by the amounts spent under rural policy. They absorbed 92 per cent of the total.' During 1987/8 £2.3 billion was spent on programmes targeted at rural England and Wales. There were 178 different forms of assistance operated by 37 agencies and no less than 94 per cent of the cash was administered by just a single body – the Ministry of Agriculture (MAFF). In addition to this staggering figure of £2.3 billion, another £450 million remains in landowners' pockets because of an exemption from paying rates on agricultural land and buildings. At one time farmers did pay rates; then in 1896 farm land was derated by 50 per cent. The Agricultural

Rates Act 1923 increased the relief to 75 per cent and since 1929 agricultural holdings have been zero-rated.

During 1977 the government did concede that in rating terms agriculture should be treated in the same way as other industries. However, it went on to reject the Layfield Committee's recommendation that farm land and buildings should logically be re-rated!

Berkeley Hill, of Wye Agricultural College, commented that although 'there were substantial sums intended to benefit the rural population in general ... these formed only a small portion of the total'. Just 2 per cent was spent by the Forestry Commission, around 1 per cent by the Rural Development Commission on social and economic measures, and the rest barely registers.

The urban–rural split in funds is equally enlightening. Stephen Hugh-Jones of *The Economist* estimates that in 1989/90 'around £775 million was spent in England on urban development programmes, while for similar work in the countryside the Rural Development Commission got only £26 million. Chapter 1 indicated that some 10 million people (one-fifth of the entire population) live and work in rural England. On a pro rata basis therefore, the £26 million should be nearer £193 million. The Duke of Westminster's inquiry into the problems of rural areas showed that in 1988/9 alone '£3,000 million was spent in Britain on the Action in the Cities programme. The new Urban Regeneration Agency will have a huge budget. Presumably much of that could have been saved if the problems of the inner-cities had been foreseen and remedial action taken earlier.' The same is true in the country – delay may prove equally costly in human and financial terms.

And while the RDC's £26 million from government (1989/90) had to be spread among those 10 million inhabitants, the Highlands and Islands secured £34 million for just 350,000 people, and the Development Board for Rural Wales, another £12.5 million to serve a population of roughly 200,000. Where is the equity in this apportionment? Stephen Hugh-Jones rubs salt in the wound by pointing out that 'the exchequer put £26 million into four occupied royal palaces; £15 million into nine royal parks and a cool £6 million for Kew Gardens'.

The Action for the Countryside programme announced by government in 1992 does include a pilot project to counter unemployment resulting from agricultural change. But it is doubtful whether the £3.6 million allocated over three years will staunch the expected haemorrhage of 30,000 such jobs over the same period.

The Tidal Wave of Rural Costs

A further problem arises because services cost more to provide and maintain in rural areas than in towns and cities. Because, of necessity, services are often small in scale they cannot make the economies of larger operations. In Suffolk, for example, a sample of 10 schools with fewer than 30 pupils exhibited unit costs which were 18–95 per cent higher than average. This was the central finding of *Counting the Rural Cost*, a report published by the National Council for Voluntary Organisations (NCVO) in 1990.

Alan Sigsworth, co-author of *The Small Rural Primary School*, is unequivocal:

> Provision of primary education in a rural area through a dispersed network of schools is expensive. Any school, however few pupils there are enrolled, incurs certain fixed costs – the building to be maintained, heated and cleaned. It is also likely that when the pupil roll is small the pupil–teacher ratio will be correspondingly low, and the cost of teachers' salaries in relation to the number of pupils therefore high.

The response from government has been to assume that significant savings can be achieved through closures. This attitude has permeated central government plans for local authority finance. County councils, as education providers, will continue to pay a heavy price if they defy Whitehall. Council tax capping and restraint on public expenditure restrict those authorities who attempt to retain their network of small schools.

Other public services are also high-cost ventures. A 1988

Monopolies and Mergers Commission report on the Post Office showed that the smallest 8,300 offices, the majority of which are rural, constitute a gross cost to the Post Office of over £4 million while the remaining larger offices actually earn £195 million.

In 1991 the Post Office acknowledged 'its special social responsibilities to rural communities', but at the same time sounded a warning about the potential effect of removing its monopoly on postal delivery. The principle of a countrywide postage rate has been adhered to for more than 150 years. It was introduced in 1840 alongside prepaid postage and the Penny Black stamp. But the 'Royal Mail estimates that the real cost of a letter to some of the most remote areas of the country is more than £1. If private companies began to cream off profitable city to city mail traffic, Royal Mail would respond to the competition.' One reaction to higher unit costs has been the introduction of part-time 'Community Offices'. As a result, since 1987 more than 100 sub offices have reopened in locations where there had been no service for some time. Somerset's Bicknoller Inn provides an unusual setting for the local office. Sue Creswell, sub-postmistress since 1988, explains that 'Whitbread were keen to develop the role of their pubs in the wider community and the games room, across the courtyard from the main building, seemed ideal for the new office.' The brewery and Parish Council clubbed together to finance conversion work. But the number of closures is still running at around 120 per year.

Higher travel costs are another burden on those serving the countryside. Take the example of a community worker moving from the London Borough of Barnet to Northumberland. In both cases the 'territory' covers around 300,000 people but the area jumps from 89 to 5,000 square kilometres. This leads to a significant proportion of 'dead time' taken up in travelling. The increase in petrol money is phenomenal and overall the cost of the service related to results is much, much higher.

Telecommunications costs, the necessarily extended timescale and slow pace of rural development, and extra expense of providing mobile or outreach facilities are further penalties. The National

Association of Citizens Advice Bureaux recognised in 1989 that their services 'take significantly longer to become established in many rural areas. The simple implication in financial terms is that costs will be higher and spread over a longer period because the work takes longer.' The ultimate and extreme rural location is provided by an island. The Isle of Wight, for example, reckons that it spends an extra £4.6 million each year to cover transport of materials by sea.

Good and Indifferent Practice

Some government and other agencies do actually compensate for higher rural costs – but the picture is erratic. In Scotland and Wales the formula for financing community health care, including district nurses and health visitors, does incorporate weighting for population sparsity, but the same does not apply in England. Government revenue support grants to local authorites take account of higher rural costs for education, but those for social services provision do not.

In the North of Scotland, customers on diesel generators pay a flat fee towards mains electricity connection. In England if the quote for mains supply is £35,000 – a not unheard of figure – then that is what the individual must find. And in rural England there are about 2,400 properties not connected to mains electricity. Peter Snart of Willow Bog Farm, near the Scottish border, is an accomplished cabinet-maker. But his business is hampered by dependence on an inadequate, expensive and unreliable generator.

Peter explains that:

> If there were two of us in the workshop, we'd be forever checking that we weren't using power equipment simultaneously – as it is I have to make sure that my wife hasn't switched on the washer when I need to use the planing machine!

If the Snarts lived in the North of Scotland Hydro-Electric Board (NoSHEB) area there would be no difficulty. NoSHEB's patch includes the Outer Hebrides, Orkney and Shetland. Since 1977 the

Company has operated an Uneconomic Rural Development Programme. The householder pays just £600 towards mains connection costing up to £10,900. If the cost of connection is greater than this the client is also liable. The arrangement was enshrined and safeguarded in the electricity privatisation legislation which went through Parliament during 1990. By contrast, in England, the customer has to shoulder a heavy financial burden. The 1988 Northumberland survey showed that quotes for mains connection ranged from £3,000 to £38,000!

A 1988 survey of households without mains services, conducted by Northumberland County Council, found that 68 respondents (82 per cent) were not happy with their generators: 'Interrupted supplies due to breakdowns and maintenance problems and high running costs are of concern to many households, as well as general inconvenience.'

Richard Butt, the Rural Development Commission's Chief Executive, has admitted that

> the lack of basic services, where it is a problem, is too big for us to tackle within our existing resources. We have asked the government to consider the case for making some modest finance available to assist remote households with the cost of connection to mains electricity . . . where this may be necessary.

During 1991 the then Junior Energy Minister, David Heathcoat-Amory, rejected this request.

The NCVO Rural Team urges agencies serving the countryside to 'build in a rural premium to compensate for higher costs. This is particularly important in the field of community care, where isolation and lack of appropriate services can make life a misery for many elderly and disabled people.' NCVO commented that 'too often the very real deprivation suffered by many people in rural areas gets overlooked. We must find ways of addressing the welfare needs of people in the country, and that starts with ensuring that adequate resources are made available.'

Rural areas have traditionally suffered from the rose-tinted images pedalled by adverts, stories such as 'Little Grey Rabbit' and treasured memories of childhood holidays in the country. The reality is much harsher. In an unpublished report commissioned during 1981 by the Department of the Environment, author Brian McLaughlin demonstrated in the Summary of Findings that 'rural areas contain a deprived population, the extent and intensity of whose disadvantage is perhaps of greater magnitude than is normally recognised'.

Population Change and the Caring Countryside

Care-in-the-community provides another example of how an image deforms policy. The rural idyll, as portrayed by Mary Russell Mitford in the 1820s, still exerts a profound influence. She described her village as 'a little world of our own . . . where we know everyone and are authorised to hope that everyone feels an interest in us'. Even if this were true in her day, the massive migration of people from the cities to the country, must surely call this into question at the end of the twentieth century. The geographer, Tony Champion, observes that 'rural districts constitute the fastest growing type of area, outpacing all other types of place in terms of both percentage and absolute size of population increase since the last Census in 1981'.

But Malcolm Moseley, ACRE's director, cautions against euphoria: 'of the 42 districts growing by more than 10 per cent between 1981 and 1991, only four lie north of the Wash. And when parish level census data emerges . . . we will certainly find scores of very small areas where depopulation continues apace.'

The 1990 General Household Survey also points to profound changes overtaking society. In 1971, one in twelve families had a single parent; by 1990 this figure was almost one in five. Also the largely rural areas of East Anglia and the South West showed that the proportion of two-car to no-car households was running neck-and-neck. This could be construed as evidence of an increasing division between the rural haves and have-nots. There is real danger in assuming that the 'rural community' is a homogeneous unchanging

Figure 2 Population movements 1981–91

Types of district	Population (thousands)	Change 1981–91 (%)
Greater London		
Inner boroughs	–147	–5.9
Outer boroughs	–172	–4.1
Metropolitan districts		
Principal cities	–370	–8.7
Other districts	–372	–4.3
Non-metropolitan districts		
Large cities	–131	–3.7
Small cities	+ 11	+0.6
Industrial areas	– 42	–0.6
New town districts	+133	+5.0
Resorts, ports and retirement areas	+174	+5.2
Urban and mixed urban/rural	+319	+3.3
Remoter, mainly rural	+366	+6.1

Source: T. Champion, 'Marching across England's green and pleasant land: the progress of counterurbanisation', Department of Geography, University of Newcastle upon Tyne, 1991

mass, undifferentiated in terms of abilities, needs and interests.

One response to these various needs has come from voluntary groups in rural communities. At the Volunteer Centre established in 1991 there is a vast array of unpaid work going on – mainly undertaken by women. Most volunteers in the country are female and most are over 40 years old. Voluntary work is not confined to flower arranging in church, but includes work on county, district and parish councils, helping with community-run transport, the local Samaritans, CAB, meals on wheels and village hall committees. The list is endless.

'Firefighting', Voluntary Activity and Deprivation

Picture-book heroes like Fireman Sam and the Trumpton Brigade affectionately portray the part-time, semi-voluntary firefighters who cover most of Britain and Northern Ireland. They were first on the scene at Flixborough, the Brighton bombing and Lockerbie disaster. Of all the fire stations in England and Wales 67 per cent are manned solely by 'retained' crews.

The 14,500 'Retained' firecrew across England and Wales come from all walks of life but share the ability to reach their fire station within four minutes. Kay Wilson's office, at the local Forestry Commission Headquarters in the border village of Bellingham, is a brisk two minutes' drive from the station. She is one of the handful of crew members who cover 107,000 hectares. Bellingham retained fire station, in common with the 1,500 others in England, must comply with Home Office regulations governing response time. In remote rural areas, firefighters must reach the scene of any accident within 20 minutes. There are progressively faster response times for towns and cities.

Maidstone-based Don Bates, founder of the Retained Firefighters Union and a fireman of 25 years' experience, explains that

> Part-time retained firefighters constitute the most economic and efficient form of fire cover – they are indistinguishable from full-time firemen, undergo identical training and use the same equipment. At 14p an hour it's hardly surprising that countries as diverse as Thailand and South Africa are looking to establish retained fire provision along British lines.

An Audit Commission report from 1986, reviewing 'value for money in the fire service' noted that 1,500 out of a total of 2,500 fire engines are entirely staffed by retained firefighters. The study stated that 10–12 retained firefighters, providing 24-hour cover every day of the year and earning around £2,500 per year, cost the council tax-payer around £25,000 to run a station with one fire engine. In contrast 'about 900 pumps (fire engines) are manned by whole time firemen' 24 hours per day, 365 days per year. Providing the normal crew of five at all times requires an establishment of about 28 firemen (for each 'pump'), at a direct cost approaching £300,000.' Don Bates stresses that 'Retained firefighters must reach the same standards of physical fitness and technical accomplishment as their full-time colleagues and they fight the same fires, only more often.' Jeffrey Ord, Chief Fire Officer for Northumberland, has expressed his frustration that many full-time firefighters 'attend too few fires to maintain operational sharpness – it is a fact that many part-time firemen attend more fires than their whole-time colleagues'.

Surprisingly, the size of community that depends on retained crews can be substantial and includes places like Godalming in Surrey (population 19,000), Newton Abbot in Devon (population 20,000) and Dorchester (Dorset) with 14,000 inhabitants.

'But', says the Audit Commission, 'by international standards the UK fire service is expensive – about double the level in some continental countries.' One reason for this is that we have twice as many full-timers per head of population than our European neighbours. While France employed 17,000 in a country of 52 million, the UK had 39,700 full-time firefighters to serve 56 million in 1986.

Don Bates explains why this should be the case. 'If you take Holland, as an example, they have 60 per cent fewer full-timers than us pro rata and five times as many volunteers; the Germans have 900,000 members of voluntary brigades while France and Italy make heavy use of volunteers, supplemented by their armies, to deal with emergencies; works fire units are another efficient continental feature which has been allowed to decline in the UK – abroad there just isn't the obsession with costly full-time crews.'

And he concludes that

It's a constant battle to recruit enough retained firefighters. The problem is that many employers are not aware of the value of the retained service and fear the disruption of losing a member of staff occasionally, without appreciating that they are gaining a highly skilled employee, with first aid training who can take charge in a crisis, is self-confident, has great pride in their work and is a real team player.

Retained fire crew obviously constitute a relatively cheap and appropriate form of rural and urban service.

A report on *English Village Services in the Eighties*, published in 1990 by the Rural Development Commission (RDC), highlighted the continuing withdrawal of country facilities. This document was a successor to the *Decline of Rural Services* study published by Rural Community Councils collectively in 1978. The earlier document identified local services 'closing on a scale which is creating serious difficulties for many rural dwellers and is causing hardship for particular groups of the population such as the young and the elderly'. At the end of the 1970s 96 per cent of Wiltshire villages had no chemist; in Suffolk 65 per cent lacked a village school and 85 per cent of Nottinghamshire communities were without a surgery. David Clark, a rural consultant, argues strongly that 'country people are entitled to just as good a service as anyone else; self-help initiatives are fine, providing they are a supplement to conventional provision, but mustn't be used as an excuse for lack of investment or closure'.

On the other hand, the rate of closure of village shops has slowed. But evidence from Northumberland counsels against complacency: many of the shopkeepers are in late middle age and do not expect to sell their business on retirement. From Essex comes another worrying development – the very smallest villages, with less than 250 population, are less likely than larger communities to even have a mobile, let alone a village, shop. One in ten post offices across the land change hands every year. And the fortunes of village shops and post offices are inextricably tied: 75% double as a post office/store.

In 1967 village schools were a feature of half of all English settlements: by 1991 40 per cent had a primary school, usually in parishes of over 500 people. David Clark detects mixed blessings: 'rural education is now much more widely valued and there is strong recognition of the community benefits; but "local management of schools" could force smaller schools to amalgamate to cope with the paperwork required'. A 1991 RDC *Survey of Rural Services* showed that only 3 per cent of England's 9,849 rural parishes had a public nursery for pre-school children – most in parishes over 1,000 population. Only 6 per cent offered day-care for the elderly and just 2 per cent catered for the handicapped – mostly concentrated in larger places of 3,000 plus inhabitants. A staggering 73 per cent of English parishes have no daily bus service.

In 1988 Howard Newby, then Professor of Sociology at Essex University, cited the Cotswold village of Shilton as nothing more than a pretty museum piece, 'a Dr Dolittle filmset from which the crew have taken a break.... The village school closed over ten years ago, the shops have gone too. The Post Office closed at the end of 1986. There is of course no public transport.... Shilton offers packaged rural life to the well-heeled and middle aged.' But this image of communities stripped of essential services runs counter to the chocolate box picture of thriving villages.

People in the countryside should not feel disadvantaged by the mere fact that they *are* living in rural areas. (emphasis added)
John Major, 6 January 1992

Duncan Scott and his colleagues unearthed hidden rural disadvantages: 'In the Peak District everywhere has a "chocolate box" image, but we found that significant numbers of people suffered serious deprivation which was usually hidden by the beauty of the area or the relative affluence of immediate neighbours.' And people seemed at a loss as to how to influence the way their villages are changing and the social and economic deprivation they experience. The research concluded that 'even more than in urban areas there seemed a real sense of political alienation about the appropriate ways to articulate grievances and seek change'.

One of the major problems for villages, like Shilton and those in the Peak, is that 'rural policy is fragmented both in its origination and implementation. There is no one government department which is responsible for rural policy and for many, rural matters form only a minor part of their activities.' This was the conclusion of work completed at Wye College. Godfrey Claff of the Peak Park Trust argues that 'agencies working in the country actually contribute to the problem of deprivation by the way in which they carry out their functions'.

Rural Development Commission: Getting a Fair Deal for Countrypeople?

Attempting to hold-the-ring is the government's Rural Development Commission (RDC) – an agency under the wing of the Department of the Environment. The Commission was established in 1909 by Lloyd George. Through advice to government and other bodies, direct action and by financing the work of others, the RDC attempts to improve social and economic conditions for those living and working in the English countryside. The bulk of the Commission's budget goes into supporting economic development in rural areas; the smaller part funds the Commission's social programme. The Commission also provides business advice to small rural firms and finances the provision of workspace in rural areas to attract businesses and thereby create new jobs. In 1990/1 75 per cent of the RDC's project funding (£11.4 million) went on the construction of rural workshops. Locally, the Commission supports the 38 rural community councils – county-based voluntary organisations in touch with 8,159 parish councils, almost 9,000 village halls and many schools, youth and other local groups. It also supports a wide range of local projects especially in Rural Development Areas. Nationally, it has targeted voluntary organisations working in rural areas or with rural voluntary organisations through its funding of the NCVO Rural Team, WI movement and the RCC's national 'umbrella' ACRE (Action with Communities in Rural England) are other beneficiaries of significant Commission support. Figure 3 shows how the Rural Development Commission's activities have changed over time.

A past-chairman in 1990 described the following philosophy for

Figure 3   (Rural) Development Commission – significant dates and actions

1909	Development Commission established.
1920	Grant aid for Women's Institutes.
1921	Rural Industries Bureau set up to advise craftsmen. First rural community council (RCC) launched (in Oxfordshire).
1925	Village halls loan fund set up. Grant aid to rural industries.
1944/5	Village halls, scheme provides 200 halls in England and Wales plus 85 in Scotland.
1948	First funding for provision of factories.
1968	Council for Small Industries in Rural Areas (CoSIRA) established – advisory service for businesses.
1973	RCC Countryside Officers begin to be appointed to work alongside village groups. Especially to promote rural self-help.
1975/6	'Action Plans' produced to encourage rural development in partnership with county and district councils.
1976/7	Commission ceases to operate in Scotland and Wales.
1981	Experimental funding for shared equity (part rent/part mortgage) housing and craft homes (combined residence and workspace).
1982	Introduction of grant scheme for refurbishment of redundant buildings to light industrial use.
1984	Greater autonomy for Commission to direct its own priorities and expenditure. Rural Development Programmes (RDPs) established in 28 English counties to foster comprehensive approach on deep-rooted social and economic problems.
1988	CoSIRA and Commission merge to become the Rural Development Commission (RDC).
1990	RDC regionalises much of its work. Two Rural Coalfield Areas adopted as additional priority areas.
1992	Pilot Countryside Employment Programmes established in three areas facing substantial job losses resulting from agricultural change.
1993	Review of priority areas.

its economic programme: he did 'not think it proper for any government to try to reverse fundamental economic trends, and it would be foolish to attempt to do so. But what government can do is temper change by softening its cutting edge.' Given the Commission's limited budget of around £40 million (1993/4) it has had to make hard decisions about how and where to direct its funding to best effect. Since 1984 the RDC has therefore concentrated its resources on 27 Rural Development Areas (RDAs) which cover a third of rural England and are areas experiencing a concentration of social and economic difficulties. More recently it has added two Rural Coalfield Closure Areas. When introducing the RDAs in 1984 the Commission made it clear that

> we are anxious to bring together those who are able to make an impact and to take action to tackle the problems. We have therefore invited the local authorities, Rural Community Councils and other agencies to draw up Rural Development Programmes (RDPs) for the RDAs . . . the RDPs will not only include bids for Commission assistance but will also show how the programmes of others can be co-ordinated to help.

Increasingly in recent years it has given greater priority to its national advisory role and to the social dimension of its work, and in particular ways of tackling the needs of disadvantaged groups in rural areas, not only in its priority areas.

The Commission has five main principles for the preparation of RDPs: project submissions from the RDAs must be

- realistic (affordable and achievable over a period of several years maximum);
- targeted (both geographically and at particular groups within RDAs);
- based on partnership (between public agencies, voluntary bodies and the private sector);
- integrated (so that activities complement and do not clash with those of other players); and

- innovative (testing new approaches, capable of replication elsewhere).

These pose a challenge to RDP Committees but, if successful, are likely to increase the impact of the Commission's funding.

The danger in this area-based approach to rural problems, is in thinking simplistically that lines on a map will contain and address all disadvantage. Brian McLaughlin argued in the 1980s that 'rural policies should be targeted at people in need' rather than at the areas in which they live. This takes us squarely back to the dangerous belief in rural well-being – the countryside is fit and healthy; problems are few and restricted to a small number of places furthest from the mainstream – and its detrimental effect on policy which the RDC and others have been seeking to counteract. In this context it is encouraging to see the RDC continuing to address national issues while concentrating its direct action on areas of greatest need and seeking to exercise greater flexibility than it has at present to apply the full range of its programmes in areas outside the RDAs if serious problems arise, at the same time recognising the fact that some problems are widely distributed across rural areas (for example, affordable housing and transport). This is reflected in several grant schemes operated by the Commission: their Rural Transport Development Fund, for example, offers financial help to establish flexible and imaginative transport schemes. In addition, since 1989, the Rural Social Partnership Fund has sought to encourage national, non-statutory organisations (like the Samaritans) to extend their activities into rural England or to increase current coverage. On the housing front the RDC 'core funds' the 'Rural Housing Trust' to operate across England's countryside and a new 'Options Land Bank Scheme' aims to secure land for the development of low cost housing for local people. All of these demonstrate a concern for people rather than areas. Mainly as a result of the effects of the recession and financial constraints on clients and partners between 1990 and 1992 the RDC underspent the money available to it. However, the RDC fully spent its budget in 1992/3, £4 million more than in 1991/2. Its budget is increasing in the next two years.

The RDC, of necessity, deals through intermediaries – councils and other bodies – acting with and for local people. It also however supports bodies which encourage and help local communities to take action themselves, as a 'top down' approach can only deliver the goods so far. Helga Jaeger, from the University of Reading, has stressed

> it is only through active local participation – learning by doing – that development work can produce sustainable local efforts, which in turn reduce the future call on scarce, outside resources. the experience of active involvement gives residents the skills and motivation to embark on further activities.

'Subsidiarity' – the devolution of power from Brussels to national government, may be a big hit with the Conservative government but it has obviously not influenced their thinking on local government reform. In 1992 they firmly dismissed the idea of parish and town councils, as the tier of local government closest to its constituents, assuming significantly greater powers than they presently do.

A Swedish rural community worker has added that 'the day we give free rein to this idea the countryside will be changed forever'. In the penultimate chapter we shall return to these issues and demonstrate how communities have taken a lead in self-regeneration.

Part two

Dealing with reality

Chapter 3

Rural Deprivation – Fact Not Fiction

For the rural poor, disdavantage is as much a matter of interlocking
deprivations as it is for the underclass of the inner cities.
Dr Mark Shucksmith, 1990

Poverty is a cause and effect of disadvantage. Mark Shucksmith of
Aberdeen University views poverty as 'a financial inability to enjoy
the everyday styles-of-living of the majority in the community.
Disadvantage and deprivation are broader concepts, embracing not
only financial inequalities but also other non-financial factors, such
as social and geographical isolation, lack of information and advice,
and powerlessness.' In 1981 Brian McLaughlin concluded that
deprivation finds 'expression in low incomes, low levels of personal
mobility and problems of access to housing and to a range of public
and private sector services'. One-fifth of the entire rural population
of England was defined as 'disadvantaged'. Deprivation and
disadvantage were found to be closely associated with low wage
earners and the elderly poor.

Low Pay in Rural Areas

Evidence from the Highlands and Islands showed male earnings
9–12 per cent below the Scottish average in 1985. Combat Poverty
(CP), a voluntary organisation, estimates that in the Irish Republic,
with a poverty line set at 50 per cent of average income, one-fifth of
rural households could be classified as 'poor', one-third if the level
were raised to 60 per cent of average income. CP also calculated that

while 4.6 per cent of employees were at risk of poverty in 1987, this figure rocketed to 35 per cent for farmers.

Work on rural deprivation in Devon also highlights low wages as the root cause of inequality: 'It is salutory to note that despite higher than average earnings overall the south-west region contains the highest percentage of men earning £100 or less per week than anywhere else on the mainland.' The Community Council for Wiltshire goes on to portray the income and expenditure in 1992 for a family of two adults and two children, on an 'average' rural wage of £130; this is illustrated in Figure 4. Outgoings quite simply exceed income. And no allowance has been made for 'necessities' such as insurance, clothing, essential repairs, car/house maintenance and TV licence. Car ownership is usually seen as a sign of wealth, but as the Devon deprivation study observes 'in rural areas this may not be a valid view. Where car ownership becomes more of a necessity as opposed to a choice, it may indeed add to overall economic deprivation rather than indicate a good income.' The 1992 *Rural Scotland Price Survey* demonstrated that the 'average price per gallon of 4 star, leaded petrol in rural Scotland was 55.47 pence compared with 47.90 pence in Aberdeen – a difference of 15.8 per cent. The rural average for unleaded petrol was 10.8 per cent greater than the Aberdeen level and 16.7 per cent higher than in Edinburgh.' Tony

Figure 4 Income and expenditure for a family in rural Wiltshire, 1992

Income		Expenditure	
Basic wage (38-hour week)	£130.00	Rent	£ 60.00
Family Credit	£ 10.28	Community Charge/ Poll Tax	£ 8.73
Child Benefit	£ 17.00	Repayments on essential	
Housing Benefit	£ 9.87	car loan of £3,000	£ 32.30
		Electricity	£ 10.00
		Food	£ 50.00
		Travelling	£ 10.00
Total	£167.15	Total	£171.03

Source: Community Council for Wiltshire, 1992.

Mackay, who has published these surveys since 1979, comments that petrol prices in rural Scotland are a matter 'of considerable debate and criticism, and no doubt that will continue until there is a substantial reduction in the differential'.

To gauge and understand rural disadvantage, measures based on norms in urban areas may have to be discarded. Dr John Wilkinson, a public health director in North Yorkshire, cites the mortality (death) rate, which is used as a proxy for morbidity (incidence of disease), as a misleading assessment which often fails 'to demonstrate any obvious disadvantage and, indeed, may tend to suggest that overall health is better in the country. There is, of course, no evidence that this is so and this merely reflects the current inadequate measures of morbidity'.

Action with Communities in Rural England (ACRE) has identified fourteen indicators of rural deprivation.

1 *Lack of local services* and facilities which those living in urban areas take for granted; for example, medical services, public telephones, banks, post offices, job centres, Department of Social Security offices.

2 *High cost of living*; for example, petrol costs, inflated prices at small village shops.

3 *Lack of public transport* or convenient access to employment, shops and other services and facilities in nearby towns. Travel time is unproductive.

4 *Lack of low-cost housing.* Many areas also have high levels of poor quality housing which lack basic amenities.

5 *Distance from sources of information*, advice and counselling, for example, citizens advice bureaux. Telephone costs may also be greater because of distance.

6 *Low incomes* for those in local employment, often with a seasonal component.

7 *Lack of local job opportunities*, especially for women without their own transport.

8 *Limited adult education* and vocational training. High costs may also apply.

9 *Inadequate social facilities*, for example, lack of readily accessible sports facilities, halls.

10 *Lack of services for particular client groups*, such as people who are elderly, disabled or long-term unemployed, carers, pre-school children and women.

11 *Lack of political influence* because of a small voter base.

12 *Lack of control* over local resources – highlighted by land ownership patterns and distance from the seat of local government.

13 *Stigma attached to certain groups of people* – perhaps because of a more traditional view of family life – such as single-parent families, unemployed people.

14 *Lack of anonymity* when visiting local personal services, such as the GP.

There can be little doubt, then, that rural deprivation is a reality infecting the lives of a substantial minority living in rural England. There are two other, specifically rural, aspects of disadvantage to be considered.

Repopulating the Countryside

Between 1986 and 1991 80 per cent of rural districts in the Republic of Ireland experienced population decline with a disproportionate loss of younger adults. In England and Wales 'results from the 1991 Census show that the fastest growing districts between 1981 and 1991 were generally remoter, rural districts. Those with the most significant decreases in the population count were generally the principal cities', according to the campaign group Business in the Community (BIC). Older, wealthier, middle class immigrants have flocked to the countryside. In-migration masks the continued loss of young locals leaving in search of work. Information from Devon shows that '15–29 year olds are proportionately more important in out-migration than in-migration, while the converse is true for the 45–64 year olds. Thus, because "counter-urbanisation" is now such a well attested population trend we should not conclude that population loss is no longer a cause of concern in rural areas.'

The BIC report contends that incomers' personal wealth and lifestyles affect many aspects of rural life. 'The most forceful impact has been on house prices and the availability of housing for the less well off. If the migrants have no need of jobs, public transport, schools or village shops, they diminish the proportion of the population which is dependent on these things and weaken the demand for them.' This leads to what the academic Howard Newby has termed 'two nations in one village', with the 'haves' and 'have nots' living cheek-by-jowl. It could be argued that those who move to the country to find a close-knit community thereby undermine the very thing they seek. Joyce Halliday studied migration in Devon during 1987/8: 'It was particularly noticeable that two predominantly migrant groups, the retired/early retirees and those moving in search of a particular lifestyle (often again more mature than average) were to be found moving into rural Devon.' These householders 'are likely to be new to the county and, in many instances, new to the countryside'.

The research organisation Mintel estimated in 1992 that 4.5 million people planned to move to the country in the next five years and a further 8.5 million would like to move but cannot because of practical or financial considerations. The main unfulfilled wish to move comes from younger, lower income, semi-skilled manual workers who are the very people least likely to afford a place in the country or to be capable of long-distance commuting. Angela Hughes of Mintel comments on the results of a 1992 survey that 'over half (54 per cent) of those who want to leave urban areas give the dirt and noise of city life as their primary reason with 45 per cent attracted by open spaces; another 22 per cent felt that country life would be less stressful'.

A government report, *Scottish Rural Life*, forecasts that 30 per cent of Scotland's population will live in rural areas by the year 2000, compared with 25 per cent in 1971.

Needy People, rather than Needy Places

Dr Mike Winter, who helped compile the Devon Deprivation Study, argues that 'there is no simple equation between economic growth and the relief of poverty and deprivation'. Poor wage levels may continue in boom areas; rapid growth can stretch existing services and infrastructure to breaking point and there will remain 'pockets' of high unemployment even where overall levels decline. A 1992 survey of key concerns facing the 100 most rural district councils in England and Wales, showed that 79 per cent of respondents identified the need for affordable homes for local people, while 77 per cent sought to encourage rural economic development, as a priority.

Mark Shucksmith believes that if 'the dimensions of rural disadvantage can be understood, and those affected can be identified, then it will be more effective to target policies at those groups and the problems which face them, rather than at the areas in which they (and many others) live.' This view is shared by Brian McLaughlin who concludes that rural deprivation is too deeply rooted and geographically spread to be cured by area-based initiatives.

Vulnerable Groups – Aspects of Disadvantage
Women in Rural Areas

> Honestly Phil, when are they going to stop chaining women to the Aga...
>
> *Jill Archer, The Archers: Radio 4, 6 September 1992*

The demands on rural women are considerable: 68 per cent of volunteers are women, and the burden of child and family care falls disproportionately on them. Women also contribute to rural society as workers; in family-run businesses; and as elected representatives: the number of female parish councillors has doubled over the last 25 years, and stood at 27 per cent in 1991. One in three new businesses are owned by women. But women in the countryside can experience considerable hardship; the Church of England's report *Faith in the Countryside*, for example, confirmed that elderly women living alone constituted the largest single category of rural poor. In rural areas 60 per cent of women do not drive. This leaves them at the mercy of poor or non-existent public transport. Lack of self-confidence, choice, and childcare may force women to turn down jobs, lower their sights or take on work not appropriate to their training and qualifications.

Jane Grant, of the National Alliance of Women's Organisations (NAWO), has commented that 'there is much women in rural areas can do individually to meet the challenges in their own lives and communities – but their effectiveness increases tenfold when they learn to network and organise with other women'. In Northamptonshire, for example, twelve women clubbed together to bulk-buy food. Those with cars made the collections, while those without saw to orders and distribution.

Women Working?

A 1991 report, *Women and Employment in Rural Areas*, highlighted 'relatively low rates of female participation in waged work' and 'a considerable dependency on part-time work'. Job security was poor, few employees had a written contract, holiday and sick pay was largely unavailable and conditions were worse for part-timers. The research identified two major barriers to women's participation in employment: childcare and transport. 'Problems related to access to and cost of transport both exacerbated childcare difficulties for women and constituted an additional constraint on their own.'

The Sorry State of Rural Childcare

Most children of working parents in Britain are cared for by members of their family. A 1984 study found that 50 per cent of pre-school children whose mother worked part-time were looked after by their fathers and 24 per cent by the child's grandmother. 'Informal childcare arrangements with relations is not, for a number of reasons, the choice many parents would prefer to make. If the option is available, though, they take advantage of it as they probably don't have access to other services at an affordable price', says Moira Stone. She completed *Rural Childcare*, a study for the Government's Rural Development Commission, in 1991; this illustrates ignorance, complacency and Dickensian practice, and the way in which rural society has failed to provide choices in rural childcare.

The difficulties in providing rural childcare are straightforward: 'Distance between home, work and existing carers; the scattered nature of demand; poor access to information about what care is available; transport difficulties; the cost of care in relation to generally low wages; lack of suitable buildings; employers' attitudes and the very small size of many firms.'

On lack of information about childcare, Peter Mottershead comments, in work for the Equal Opportunities Commission, that 'many parents have struggled to find out what childcare is available, thinking that lack of information was the problem, only to discover that lack of childcare itself is the problem' is too often true in rural areas.

Employers' attitudes also leave a lot to be desired – in the Bude and Holsworthy area of Devon/Cornwall, Moira Stone observed that the suggestion that employers or councillors might have anything to do with childcare was frequently met with laughter. On industrial estates a more important priority is thought to be the provision of skips.

In spite of the fact that the total number of people under 25 in the employment market is projected to fall by 1.2 million between 1987 and 1995, that the population of children will rise by 12 per cent and that women with pre-school children are the fastest growing group in the workforce, there is a desperate lack of childcare nationally, but more particularly in the countryside. The *Rural Childcare* report argues that women already contend with a barrage of obstacles on returning to work – training needs, discrimination, hostile working environment, structure of the working day and negative attitudes, in many rural areas, to working women. But arranging childcare and juggling the responsibilities of working parents is seen as the biggest and most common difficulty.

The list of childcare options is legion but most, in practice, are 'off limits' for rural children. In addition to care by relations there is childminding, private day, workplace and community nurseries, mothers' helps and au pairs, playgroups for toddlers, nursery schools, creches, out of school and holiday activities and childcare subsidies. But there are gaps in provision. Most local authority day nurseries are primarily for those 'at risk', and they are a rarity in rural areas. Britain has publicly funded childcare for less than 2 per cent of children under 3, in marked contrast to 44 per cent for Denmark. Even Portugal provides for 4 per cent of children under 3 years. In the entire country there are only some 120 workplace nurseries, offering 3,000 places, mostly in hospitals, colleges, local authorities and a few in the private sector. Most are in towns and cities and, during the recession employers have closed nurseries both to cut costs and because they do not need to woo women back into work.

Nationally, playgroup places are available to 13 per cent of under fives. Only 23 per cent of 3 and 4 year olds attend local authority nursery classes or schools. There are not enough places in most areas and only a few provide all-day cover. Out-of-school care is virtually out of the question. 'Only one primary school child in 538 has a place in an out-of-school hours care scheme which looks after children and provides activities and tea until the parent can collect them. There are no schemes in the majority of rural counties', says Moira Stone.

What is certain is that more money is needed to make schemes like these more readily available.

Gillian Shepard, MP, Employment Secretary, 1992

In 1992 the National Council for Voluntary Childcare Organisations – a charitable 'umbrella' for concerned bodies such as the national voluntary organisation Kids' Clubs Network (KCN) – launched a three-year rural childcare initiative. Jointly funded by the RDC and Department of Health the project aims to disseminate examples of good practice and draw on experience from Europe. Grant aid is also available to support a series of practical 'demonstration' projects.

KCN showed in 1990 that outside London, only 2.5 per cent of schools ran an out-of-school scheme, while 'a fifth of schools say that there is a demand'. In spite of this, the vast majority of schools had no plans to provide cover and over 'three-quarters of schools agreed that some funding would need to be identified before they could set up a scheme'. KCN established a rural project in 1992 with funding from the RDC, Calouste Gulbenkian Foundation and one other charitable trust. Rural development officer, Alison Marshall, is working on a national basis, while conducting action research in North Yorkshire, Cornwall, Shropshire, mid-Bedfordshire, Suffolk and Dorset to 'raise the profile of the needs of school age children for decent childcare in rural areas. The emphasis is on children's needs, and with enabling women to return to work.' KCN hopes to boost the number of rural out-of-school schemes, conduct action research and publicise examples of best practice, over the two-year life of the project.

Examples of good practice are few and far between, but there are some. In Trowbridge, Wiltshire, the day nursery at Bowyers (the meat-pie manufacturers) has been in operation as a non-profit making organisation for nearly 20 years.

Manuscript Ltd of Liskeard (Cornwall) employs around 100 people, most of whom are women, producing framed pictures for large chainstores. The firm operates a 16-place workplace nursery as a means of limiting the loss of trained women workers when they have children. The nursery caters for children up to 5 years and is located in a specially adapted wing of the factory. Set up costs were £25,000 plus £5,000 for equipment; running costs are about £30,000 per year. Their efforts resulted in the reappointment of six previously trained workers.

Ann Watts of the Midland Bank Group, which estimates an annual loss of £14 million per annum because of trained staff leaving, has observed that help with childcare 'is not just an employment issue, it's about the profitability of the company, it's about the bottom line'.

The North West Leicestershire Rural Childcare Scheme offers very different assistance in the form of vouchers paid to registered carers. This initiative, launched in March 1992, via the local Council for Voluntary Service, aims to 'bridge the financial gap between unemployment and employment for women returners or single parents; enable them to take up training or paid work, thereby enhancing their quality of life and increasing the standard and amount of childcare in North West Leicestershire'.

Parents receiving one of a range of benefits (for example, income support) can claim vouchers for up to two children under 12 years of age. These childcare tokens are worth 50p each per hour per child and can be used for a maximum of 30 hours per week, spread over 24 weeks in the year. Parents are able to choose from a range of options including registered childminders, creches or members of the family. By September 1992 31 parents had received assistance through the scheme.

The other side of the Leicestershire project is training for the people in the voucher system who are providing childcare. Malcolm Flaherty, the scheme's development officer, hopes that 'as more childcare providers receive training, so there will be a greater availability of this resource for people returning to work or further education to choose from'.

Alison Marshall believes that there is still a long way to go before rural areas can boast reasonable childcare facilities: without decent childcare assistance there is a 'vicious circle' where women cannot return to work because of inadequate childcare provision, and provision is inadequate because women have low economic status. Despite interest and a degree of enthusiasm among some rural employers and others, the majority are waiting for someone else to take the initiative towards the development and management of childcare which is suitable and affordable. Many women work out of financial necessity or to break down the isolation of rural life. Lack of childcare options can lead to costly and sometimes debilitating choices. Working women in rural areas may also face personal 'attacks' based on the stereotype of uncaring women, abandoning their children to a stranger, but for children this contact can be enriching and can boost their social skills.

Childcare is only one aspect of the lot of women in rural areas. Women have differing needs, attitudes and aspirations, for which a range of options must be offered. Their concerns will change over time – as children grow up or as parents age. The hopes and expectations of different generations of women will also vary.

Accessibility and Low Pay

The *Women and Employment* study points to a complicated 'juggling act' involving women's domestic and working lives. Access becomes 'not simply a function of transport provision but relates also to time, money and the ability to co-ordinate daily activities'. With regard to pay it was clear that most women received relatively low wages. More detailed information, from the Northern Region Low Pay Unit, confirms that while 57 per cent of Northumberland's workforce earns below the European Decency Threshold, the incidence is twice as high for female workers (78.5 per cent) as for males (38.1 per cent). In 1990 nearly half of all full-time working women in Northumberland earned less than £150 per week.

Lone Parents

Karen Richardson is a single parent with a four year old daughter. Since 1991 she has co-ordinated a 'One-parent families rural support project', based in York. The scheme is hosted by the charity One-Parent Families, and is also affiliated to the national agency, Gingerbread. Most of Karen's clients are women, who can experience 'extreme geographical and social isolation; non-existent access to information and support services; "invisibility" to decision-makers and endemic poverty. One woman lives on income support in a council house, has a child without a bed, washes all the clothes by hand and manages with a broken cooker.'

Help for Rural Lone Parents provides minibus collection to and from monthly drop-in sessions, home visits from an Advice Worker and supervised play for children. Karen sees the project as a responsive, democratically organised, self-help scheme.

A Tale of Two Disabilities

I remain convinced that I am more handicapped by my
environment than by my disability.

Linda Hoggarth, Chair, mid-Suffolk Rethink for Disabled
People, 1991

Robert Arckless radiates quiet confidence and a sense of mission. At
34 he is a town, district and county councillor representing Amble, a
former coalport of 6,000 inhabitants. He lives with his mother, now
55, who is plagued by epilepsy and heart trouble. 'I was very shy as a
youngster and was brought up in an entirely adult household. I was
what is known in educational jargon as an "isolate" – not a good
person to mix with at school', says Robert. His grandfather made an
indelible impression on him.

He was a miner who lost an eye in a pit explosion; he loved
books and was a real 'fire-in-the-belly socialist'. During the
1926 General Strike he was arrested for trying to derail the
Flying Scotsman, which was carrying coal up and down the
country. He died when I was 21, following a very long illness
and succession of strokes. He was my male role model.

Grandfather Arckless instilled in the young Robert a love of
books, a zeal for self-improvement and the desire to help others.

I'm not a theoretical socialist – I just want to make society
better than it is. When I first became a councillor, eight years
ago, I was a bit starry-eyed. Since then there have been large
doses of reality – you can't wave a magic wand and a small
authority is pretty limited in what it can achieve in terms of
public housing, economic development and job creation.

It's best to be straight with people; to tell the truth even if it
isn't popular. As a councillor you can make a real contribution
to improving people's lives. One family I visited were in a
council house without heating and the place hadn't been
rewired or painted for years. It turned out that an
administrative slip-up had lumped their property in with a

newer development – so the officers were convinced that there wasn't a problem. As the go-between, I was able to settle the matter and the work was done.

I was especially pleased with the construction of a sheltered housing scheme for local elderly and disabled people in Amble. It was a big project, difficult to get off the ground and to sustain. The District Council brought the project off well and should be proud of it. What made it special was the degree of collaboration between the County Social Services and Area Health Authority.

Counselling Against Despair

This may all seem run-of-the-mill stuff for any councillor. But there's something that picks Robert Arckless out from the crowd. He's disabled. As a toddler he fell down stairs and has suffered the effects ever since. Robert's cerebral palsy means that the right side of his body is partially paralysed.

The physical problems are intruding more with age. I experience muscle spasms and a fair bit of pain. My optician was less than enthusiastic when I asked him about driving and pretty much told me that my short-sightedness was on a par with Mr Magoo! The paralysis is like having a sheet of cloth permanently lodged under the skin.

Although my disability did close off some options, it encouraged my pleasure in reading – my mind is free and active even if my body sometimes lets me down.

There are particular problems of being disabled and living in the countryside. Rural jobs are few and far between, so if an employer has two evenly matched candidates the disability may just tip the scales the other way.

The Spastics Society confirmed in 1992 that disabled applicants for jobs were still being discriminated against. The Society continues to advocate that disabled people should be accorded legal rights to employment. Small to medium-sized businesses – which are the mainstay of rural areas – were the worst offenders. The reasons for rejecting volunteer job-hunters sent out by the society ranged from fears that a disabled staff member would be a disruptive influence to a false assumption that disability equalled inefficiency.

Robert Arckless went for an interview in Newcastle-upon-Tyne (about 1½ hours by bus) and the job looked promising.

> But to reach the office I had to negotiate three subways and cross a busy main road. By the time I arrived I was absolutely shattered. And the buses are another problem in rural areas. I depend on public transport which can be quite expensive and take you 'round the houses' to your destination.
>
> It was rather ironic in 1990 because the Department of Employment decided to close Amble Jobcentre (along with 800 across the country) and centralise their services. When our delegation met representatives from the Department I was able to say 'I'm a county councillor and recipient of the service.' It still didn't change their minds. Given the choice of climbing two flights of stairs in Amble or taking the bus and then walking to the Jobcentre at Alnwick, I'd prefer the local facility every time.
>
> My first bout of unemployment started in 1980 and lasted four years. I felt very bad about that.

Robert has a degree in History and English and a post-graduate certificate in education. He has started a computer training course after a second spell out of work.

> We managed with difficulty – from overdraft to overdraft. If it hadn't been for my mother's widow's pension I don't know where we'd have been. From the cost point of view it's just as well that I'm a home bird, love books and don't go out much. My councillor's attendance allowance is erratic although it has increased with elevation to vice-chair of the county's economic development sub-committee. Everyone who wants to make a contribution as a councillor should be enabled to do so. The DSS virtually said to me that I should resign from the county

council, so that I could receive £44 a week unemployment benefit. I said I'd see them in hell first!

And what of the future? 'My greatest personal fear is in becoming less mobile – only being able to reach the end of the street. And as far as my council work is concerned, I've gone further than I ever expected. Mind you, the longer you're in local government the more people you upset!'

Handicapped but not Disabled

Baroness Masham lives on the edge of a small town in North Yorkshire. It has a community hall

> which to me and my wheelchair is inaccessible. The town has two banks, a Post Office – all inaccessible; there is a library up a flight of stairs, above the Midland Bank. In fact none of the social amenities, apart from the pubs, is accessible to anyone in a wheelchair.

Councillor Robert Arckless with Amble Marina behind
(Duncan Davis)

> I compare my daily living with that of my husband. He could, if he wanted, ride a bicycle, or take the postbus – which is the only public transport out of the village. But if you have no other means of travel and are wheelchair-bound, how do you get onto the postbus in the first place?

She cites the closure of village services, as well as the physical layout of buildings, as formidable barriers preventing people who are disabled from gaining access to facilities. During 1986 Baroness Masham piloted a Disabled Consultation Bill through Parliament, parts of which remain to be implemented. One of these is an unbelievably simple and basic requirement to find out who the disabled people are and where they live.

Incontinence is a particular problem for para and tetraplegics and for many elderly people. If incontinence goes unchecked it can lead to complications and secondary infections. An associated problem is that of waste disposal. In urban centres there is likely to be a collection service which gets rid of waste items but this is not always the case in rural areas.

> Not so long ago I nursed someone with AIDS and you can imagine how critical the question of disposal was.... The majority of people will be totally unaware of these difficulties ... pressure should be brought to bear on local authorities to provide this service for people suffering incontinence.
>
> Physical disabilities are very complicated. The needs of one type may be totally different from another.... This is what makes health care provision so difficult in rural areas and why there is real fear among country people of becoming disabled. For example, many rural GPs never see a paraplegic like me, and I know of many other cases in which almost intractable problems arise because of being resident in a rural areas – a young man that I know with severe diabetes and going blind has to travel enormous distances to get rehabilitative treatment.

Do the community and relief agencies exist locally to provide essential back-up? Not all voluntary organisations can, or are able to, reach far into the countryside. Problems may also exist in attracting experienced, specialist, staff to work in rural areas. This is especially true in the remedial professions,

> speech and physiotherapy, for example, where there are problems nationaly in meeting staffing levels. Those who are at work in the country are often overstretched in trying to cope with demand.
>
> How to communicate information and advice about the availability of health, personal social service and voluntary agency assistance is a real issue in rural provision. Often it is not because the needs cannot be met but rather that the person in need, patient or professional, does not know to whom or where to turn.

Mental Health in Rural Areas

As many as one in five people suffer some sort of mental distress during their lives for which they receive medical treatment. However, recent statistics show that farmers and agricultural workers are second only to doctors as most likely to take their own lives.

A clear-cut picture of rural ill-health emerges from a review of mental illness and suicide, although it is a powerful myth to believe that those who commit suicide must be mentally ill. Di Stubbs, of the Samaritans Rural Outreach team, estimates that in the UK 'four farmers a week are taking their own lives and farmers are twice as likely as the general population to commit suicide'. Financial pressures such as falling land values and farm incomes, effect of quotas and the threat of foreclosure are frequently mentioned as the main factors leading to despair and suicide. For the farmer – usually a man – there are other factors which conspire to make life unbearable: for those without a family there is the effect of often cripplingly long hours and return to an empty farmhouse; isolation of the job; the stress of 'keeping up appearances' and lack of time or opportunity to find support. Di Stubbs also cites 'responsibility to previous generations – if David Archer fails, he doesn't just let himself down, he lets down Phil, Peggy, Dan and Old Dan'.

The Duke of Westminster, at the launch of a pioneering mental health venture, aimed at agricultural communities in Herefordshire, commented that it was 'ironic that those in rural areas are doing something worse than rioting. They are killing themselves. They are doing it quietly and it doesn't make headlines.' In response, in the late 1980s the Samaritans launched a rural outreach programme. Their work has spurred others to develop counselling services in rural areas.

Mental health needs are cloaked by society's sense of discomfort with the unhappiness and abnormal behaviours defined as 'mental illness'. Community care proposals have brought to a head the social dis-ease with disempowered groups who live temporarily or permanently in a reality that others cannot, will not or are too frightened to interpret.

Typically, provision for the mentally ill involves initial contact with General Practitioners (GPs) who may prescribe drugs, counselling or referral to specialist staff, including psychiatrists, psychologists, community psychiatric nurses, day or residential units. What does this mean in practice?

Ann's Story

Ann, a professional woman in her thirties, still has strong feelings about the care she received for clinical depression, latterly diagnosed as benzodiazepine (BZ) addiction and subsequent withdrawal.

I assumed the role of a mentally ill person for about three years. During this time I attended my GP's surgery regularly despite his evident inability to do much more than ascertain that it still hurt. The doctor ladled out a ferocious combination of drugs as if there was a chemical solution to any problem. He accepted that I was travelling long distances to the surgery, when probably far from clear headed due to medication. But my GP failed to give adequate direction about tolerance and addiction with BZs, threatened me with compulsory hospital admittance if I didn't go voluntarily and referred me to a unit he had never even visited. He also insisted that I continue drug therapy even though I wanted to stop. I had no one to turn to for advice and could see no real alternative in an area covered by a small practice. It all comes down to choices and access and I don't feel I had either.

In terms of choices, Ann was registered with a rural practice eight miles by car from her cottage and inaccessible by public transport. The two male GPs had no enhanced psychiatric or counselling skills. Country practitioners can have lists covering a vast territory. 'I hated talking when I knew there were others wanting to see the doctor – pills satisfied his need to be doing something for me although it was not what I needed or wanted. And a house call would have monopolised the only doctor on call.' Choice of consultant was also limited by referral patterns particular to the practice. 'It was tough if you needed support to make changes to how you think and behave, when the consultant specialised in chemotherapy . . . and all you can do is trust the information you're given about pills.' Ann lived more than 20 miles from the nearest library and almost 30 from voluntary groups giving encouragement and advice. 'Even the phone calls were all long distance – and me on sick pay!' Community-based care or convalescence is little easier, with 50-mile round trips, for the community psychiatric nurse she never got to see, one client monopolising half a day of which only an hour might involve actual contact.

This also highlights problems about access, always involving car travel in her home area, often over considerable distances and under the influence of prescribed drugs. One advantage of distance, however, is that rural GPs can register as dispensing practices, so that tablets are available before leaving the premises, but in this case in full view of other patients waiting to make appointments with the receptionist. Ann spent two or three hours travelling to specialists for a session of ten minutes to an hour. This procedure 'consumed whole days, focused on either being or feeling ill or seeking a cure'. Access is also a problem for visitors. 'I was hospitalised across the county. While it gave me anonymity, it also made me virtually inaccessible except by car; public transport would have involved friends travelling for the best part of a day.' She also found herself in an industrial area, very different from her own, agricultural environment: 'I didn't share the vocabulary or experiences of the majority of people there; I was ostracised for days for being an undercover doctor put on the ward to spy! However fatuous it may sound now, it added greatly to my sense of isolation and made an unpleasant set of circumstances absolutely wretched.'

Practice and Good Practice

Ann's story highlights the failure of urban models of service provision to provide for small, scattered communities and the individuals who live there. However, there are examples of new initiatives, many of which share principles of good practice.

Yorkshire and Trent Health Authorities, for example, avoid the use of stigmatising labels such as the 'Friday Depression Group', preferring instead more general terms. They say services should ideally cater for a broad range of needs, including adult education relaxation classes and wider mental health questions. They should draw on known and acceptable support from specialist counselling bodies and encourage contact with carers who have had similar experiences. Accessibility is vital both in terms of anonymity and public transport services.

Voluntary organisations have considerable potential to respond and develop models of delivery. There is a desperate need to invest in rural development workers and the existing infrastructure. Harnessing the catalytic potential of voluntary agencies requires stable, often modest, funding and specialised training; time required to mobilise and involve the local community must be allowed for. But Jan Sherlock of the national agency Good Practices in Mental Health (GPMH), suspects that rural GPs tend not 'to take the voluntary sector seriously, so are unlikely to refer to them or to self-help initiatives which constitute a good rural approach'. People need to know what is available to them – this is best done through the establishment of a comprehensive and accurate data base. Self-help in rural areas occurs through a variety of channels rather than the urban model of single-problem mutual-aid groups. Use of existing transportation and opportunities, plus an exploration of how to bring services to the people, including countering the centralisation of services as a result of investment choices, are all issues that must be addressed if rural mental health provision is to be adequate and appropriate for those who need it.

Northern Causeway to Mental Health

Sheila Dixon sits calmly among piles of bric-a-brac, potted plants and the odd hockey stick. This is her 'office'. She is straightforward in dealing with one issue that remains off limits in social chit-chat.

> Manic depression gives you the feeling of losing touch with reality. At times I was imagining the strangest catastrophes. When we were in the Highlands I can actually remember ringing my friends in the middle of the night to warn them that a tidal wave was on its way. I recognise the danger signals now and, with the help of tablets, can usually keep it at bay. The point is that even when I am 'off the beam', it's doubtful that anyone would notice – the real conflict is going on inside.

Sheila, 39, has turned her experiences of mental illness to positive effect – co-ordinating a rural community project for the Northern Schizophrenia Fellowship (NSF). Since March 1991 she, and an assistant, have established a series of drop-in centres for those at risk, experiencing, or recovering from mental illness. Three-hourly sessions are held twice weekly in the communities of Belford, Seahouses and Wooler – larger villages in England's northernmost borough of Berwick upon Tweed. Sheila observes that

> since their launch around 25 volunteers and 37 sufferers have attended; most are elderly or middle-aged women and we are

*Sheila Dixon counselling at the Northern Causeway
Project Office, Belford, Northumberland
(Duncan Davis)*

now particularly keen to get through to younger peope. There's a broad range of illness – one unfortunate man was struck on the head by a circular bale, and ever since has heard voices and been unable to hold down a job; another lady moved from the city and, shortly after, her husband died. She's become so lonely that she sometimes wanders down to the harbour, hoping to meet a coach of day-trippers from Edinburgh.

When the project was searching for funds it stressed that 'self-help, voluntary input and education through involving the local community are important to the philosophy of the NSF'. So how have the people of Belford reacted to the Causeway office and drop-in centre? It's neatly tucked behind a supermarket, adjacent to a small caravan park and forestry depot. 'There's no open hostility but on the other hand, so far, there is limited, active support. I think most people feel that it's all very worthy and well intentioned but nothing to do with them personally', says Sheila. A central goal of Northern Causeway is to break down the prejudice and ignorance that affect views of mental distress. 'Somehow people make a strong distinction between physical complaints, treatment and recovery, and mental illnesses – loneliness, stress and depression. There may be a fear that it's "catching" or that it's tantamount to being a violent psychopath', contends Sheila Dixon.

So far the drop-in sessions cover a range of creative and supportive activities including weaving, quizzes, yoga for relaxation, rug-making, advocacy, socialising and befriending, sports and social outings. What happens is very much in the hands of those who come along. The project has also launched its own *Link Up* newsletter. This offers practical tips as well as humour. 'Life is a sexually transmitted disease which is invariably fatal!' Or 'the reason that you don't understand me, Edith, is that I'm talking in English and you're listening in Dingbat.' Alternatively, by way of encouragement, 'Happiness is like a butterfly. The more you chase it, the more it will elude you. But if you turn your attention to other things, it comes and softly sits on your shoulder.' All this may sound frivolous but it conveys the germ of a deadly serious objective: 'To provide facilities, support and assistance for those who suffer from schizophrenia and other allied illnesses and for their families, dependants and carers. Also to increase public awareness of what it means to live with mental illness in the family or the community.' A number of agencies have backed these aims with around £40,000 spread over two years: Northumberland Health Authority, St Hilda's Charitable Trust, the Rural Development Commission and Charity Projects are among the co-funders. And what of the barriers? Sheila Dixon has been initially 'disappointed with the lukewarm attitude of local GPs towards the initiative. It would be a major breakthrough to have them as active participants.' So far most people have referred themselves and just turn up at one of the centres. The community psychiatric nursing (CPN) team has lent valuable support. On the positive side, their Dutch landlord offered a wall near the project office: for Mental Health Awareness Week he requested a 'controversial' mural ('not just trees or a landscape'). He has also held out the possibility of flexible, paid, forestry work for those attending Northern Causeway.

The project has an active and representative steering group made up of a consultant psychologist, parish councillor, manic depressive, community psychiatric nurse, volunteer helper, family doctor and social worker. Sheila states her approach quite simply: 'We start with people's needs and work from there; it's quality of service that's of paramount importance and not quantity.' Sheila understands the meaning of mental illness in a rural setting from bitter personal experience. For 10 years she and her husband ran a busy village shop, near Ullapool in the Scottish Highlands. 'Running the store completely took us over. We had no time to ourselves and became everybody's servant, delivering here, there and everywhere. My breakdown was a bit like a fusebox blowing – something of a self-protection mechanism.'

Sheila Dixon recognises that they have a long road ahead in trying to change ingrained attitudes: 'One volunteer to the project even questioned whether rural residents really suffered mental health problems! With all that peace and quiet around she concluded that it could only be put down to one thing – that certain individuals were weak willed.' Sheila scoffs at the memory and turns her attention to more constructive pursuits.

Bassetlaw Befriending

Bassetlaw MIND, a charity operating in rural Nottinghamshire, believes that community mental health provision should be 'based on the principles of individual dignity, respect and concern; it should be free of charge, local, accessible and flexible enough to respond to changing needs and circumstances'.

Since 1986 Bassetlaw MIND has been enacting these ideals through its Befriending Programme. Friendship, support and social activities are offered to those in need of company. Befrienders work to an agreed outline – setting boundaries to a relationship, observing confidentiality and accepting regular supervision and support. Once the volunteer is matched with a 'client' an informal contract is drawn up and reviewed every few months. The arrangement is also seen as providing two-way benefits: Kevin, a volunteer, plays 'badminton and other sports – it's not really competitive, just for enjoyment. We meet once a week which suits us well and keeps us both fit.'

Rachel was befriended and, when she started to feel better, decided to

> put something back after receiving so much. I attended a volunteer course and really enjoyed it as well as learning a great deal.
>
> I now befriend someone myself...there are times when I wonder if I am doing it right, but I know that MIND is at the end of the 'phone for support and guidance.... I am very aware of confidentiality and how important it is. Things said to my volunteer were treated in confidence and the lady I visit knows she will receive the same respect.

Befriending schemes must vigorously insist on confidentiality, because in rural areas people can be very visible. If befrienders are drawn from outside their clients' own locality, this can assist towards maintaining confidentiality.

A community psychiatric nurse working with the scheme comments that the

> people that I have referred have been very isolated and lacking in confidence. They've been vulnerable and have had depleted relationships because of happenings in their past. The befriender can fill a social role that I neither have the time for, nor is it in my brief. The people referred by me need someone as a friend – to value them.... I shall continue to make use of the service.

Review and Preview

The Bassetlaw initiative is tackling a major cause of relapse and re-admission – loneliness. Jan Sherlock acknowledges that 'newcomers to a village and single elderly residents can suffer acute isolation and communities can be intolerant of anyone who stands out as "odd" or "different" '. GPMH concludes that in general

> services in rural areas suffer the same fate as the people they seek to help; they are cut off, have to meet multiple needs through a single resource and they tend to be viewed as less important than those in urban areas. People planning services must recognise this by allocating sufficiently generous travel budgets and support for isolated workers. The Good Practices in Mental Health rural initiative puts marginalised rural practitioners in touch with colleagues working in similar ways.

Young People in Rural England

Dave Phillips of the National Youth Agency (NYA) contends that 'the predominant, adult, view of young people in rural areas is too often concerned with the problems they are perceived to cause rather than the legitimate needs that they have because of where they live'.

Young people face real pressures within rural communities. The 'goldfish bowl' of small village life makes everything so public; friendship patterns are narrow and unorthodox dress and behaviour tend to be frowned upon. This can all add up to a bitter cocktail of isolation, claustrophobia, limited horizons, low self-esteem and poorly developed personal identity. Jerry Smith, a community development worker in Norfolk, believes that 'boredom is a significant factor for rural youth... in many villages, there is just nothing for young people to do – and how do you participate, with nothing to participate in?' Dependence on parents to provide transport and little or no influence on local decision-making are further problems for young people in the countryside.

Evidence from southwest England adds a twist to the picture of child–parent dependency. Researcher Claire Wallace found a number of young people 'socialised into long hours, hard work and poor rewards...the dependence of young people upon the family was balanced by the dependence of the family upon them: under some circumstances the young person's labour could be a crucial part of the family business'. This pattern was reinforced by the high incidence of small businesses and self-employment in the rural southwest.

Central to an improved quality of life for young people in rural areas, is the idea of joint working by agencies and building on the ideas and needs expressed by young people themselves.

Access to the Levers of Power

In North Cornwall a job applicant sits across the table from an interview panel. The prize – a youth work post covering Bude and Launceston. Questions are fired by a range of people – all aged 14–17 and regulars at the centre where part of the work will be based. The outgoing worker, Trevor Crawley, wanted to see whether it was possible to devise an interview which reflected young people's concerns and drew them into the selection process. He was at pains not to create an 'elite group', and also to avoid throwing young people in at the deep end.

The agreed format was a half-hour interview conducted by young people with each candidate, followed by a buffet lunch. Their preference was then relayed to a parallel, adult selection committee which itself included one young person. Gareth, then aged 15, takes up the story:

> It was a new experience to find out what an interview is like. I'll have to go for an interview for a job when I leave school next year and it will be really useful. I learnt a lot – how to get an answer by asking a question indirectly, organisational skills, how to work in a group and make decisions.... I think youth workers should be interviewed by young people – that's who they are going to be working for.

The young people's representative on the formal interview panel, James Bailes, was treated in exactly the same way as the rest of the panel; the only difference was that he had to complete all his detentions, for smoking and skateboarding, before he could have the day off school to attend.

Trevor Crawley concluded that the

interviews were handled in a mature and disciplined way. Continuity and timekeeping were exemplary. James's involvement on the main panel was applauded . . . . And what about the final result? Was the young people's choice the one that prevailed? The answer is 'yes' – because they made the same choice as the adults, and for very much the same reasons.

'On Yer Bike'

As a young man lay dying in hospital from injuries sustained in a motorbike crash, Reg Hallam – a local printer – felt that something must be done to prevent further tragedies. The result has been the Peak Dale Youth and Motorcycle Club, with over 1,500 members – 400 actively participating in 1992 – and a further 40 adults and 'graduate' members as marshals and supporters.

Angie Corby, of Derbyshire RCC, describes Peak Dale (population: 750), which is the focus for this club, as 'a street with 10 quarries. It's not a pretty place but reclamation work is gradually improving things. Lorries thunder through and the National Park boundary skirts the village.'

The club offers training for 4–18 year olds in bike handling! Each member takes out their own insurance while the club has a stock of bikes for individual use. This helps people who can't afford their own machine and can avoid needless expense in those cases where someone's interest wanes after a while. There are 'nursery' classes, provision for scrambling, and the next step is a garage/workshop to encourage motorbike maintenance and all-weather use of the old quarry.

The original caravans have given way to a proper HQ complete with canteen, toilets (including one for disabled people), registration and storage areas. Angie Corby comments that it's a 'self-build, self-scrounge enterprise, now valued at £50,000. Members have used every opportunity to raise money, or find materials – many of these items have been recycled and put back to productive use.' The Sports Council, Rural Development Commission, High Peak Borough and Wormhill Parish Council and a local trust plus numerous nearby businesses have all chipped in.

Somehow Reg Hallam manages a full-time job and, along with the Club's supervisors, organises motorbike training by night and at weekends. St John's Ambulance plan to run first-aid courses on site for members. At a later date permission may be sought for jet skiing on one of the soup green quarry 'lakes'.

Angie Corby measures the success of Peak Dale Youth/Motorcycle Club in the following terms: 'The quarry is a self-contained crater, so there is no noise or nuisance for surrounding properties; young people gain a respect for speed and understand the importance of road safety. It's a constructive channel for youthful enthusiasm.'

Looking Ahead

The NYA's Dave Phillips admits that the 'days of the one-night-a-week village youth club are not over, but where they can be complemented by information and advice work, the introduction of new activities and a genuine understanding of young people's concerns, then perhaps young people in rural areas will cease to be the ones whose needs are remembered last'.

'Out' in the Country

In London's gay community, Village Youth is one of the 'pink pound's' success stories of the 1990s. Opened some three years ago as a bar off Tottenham Court Road, the company now has three bars in central London – and full-page ads in the gay press plugging the rural idyll – two young men, stripped to the waist, in their early twenties, with designer bodies, strolling across the idealised rural landscape, corn stooks waving, combine buzzing, not a care in the world. In London, at least, many gay men share the aspirations of their 'straight' contemporaries – get rich, get back to your rural roots, keep two lifestyles (the home in the country, the job in the city – the best of both worlds).

The reality for gay men living outside the big cities (and for lesbians too, although they are still less visible in the country than they are in the city) is very different. The commercial gay scene – pubs, discos, clubs – is less developed, and tends to concentrate on one venue in larger towns, or an occasional weekly or monthly disco. More informal networks do exist – gay community organisations in county towns, telephone support and counselling services such as Friend, and networks of individuals (such as Border Women in the Welsh Marches). If you know where to look, and what to look for, you can meet other lesbians and gay men. Not surprisingly, it's harder to be anonymous in rural areas, where non-conforming behaviour can sometimes be less acceptable. Lesbians and gay men often report harassment from other people living in the same village or town; there tend to be fewer positive role models for younger people coming to terms with their sexuality and it can be harder to identify sources of support.

The 'system' is less friendly too. Those local authorities which have adopted high profile lesbian and gay units, working inside and outside the council structure to challenge discrimination, have all been in large cities. Allocation of council housing, policies on youth and community work and grant aid to local groups seem to deny the existence of lesbians and gay men in the rural context. In Herefordshire, a group of women reported that a local authority had forbidden use of one room in a building owned by a voluntary organisation (but grant-aided by the Council) for fear of being seen intentionally to promote homosexuality. Another local authority in Hereford and Worcester nearly failed to fund a community building in Worcester because part of it was used by a telephone helpline for lesbians and gay men.

No wonder, then, that many lesbians and gay men leave the village/town they were brought up in, and move (if they can) to the city where it's easier to be anonymous, and where the pressures to conform are less acute. Those who stay need a car, a telephone, the independence of a good job and regular income to afford to buy a piece of the rural idyll. The quandry is well expressed by a gay switchboard in the Midlands.

> The opportunities to get accurate information, meet others and get personal support are very limited by low income, isolation, and lack of personal access to transport. The facilities are many miles away in a major town, often late at night only. One caller... was so depserate to meet others socially he paid £10 for a private hire car one way.

That many lesbians and gay men do achieve a personal sense of well-being in rural areas is more to do with the strength of their support and character than with the traditional 'caring' image of rural communities. It is also, as much as anything, a sign that rural communities are not immune to change and that the new heterosexual population, in search of its own rural idyll, has brought with it a greater degree of tolerance.

Race and Rural Areas

The price seemed reasonable, location
Indifferent. The Landlady swore she lived
Off premises. Nothing remained
But self-confession. 'Madam,' I warned
'I hate a wasted journey – I am African,'
Silence...
'ARE YOU DARK? OR VERY LIGHT?' Revelation came.
'You mean – like plain or milk chocolate?

From Wole Soyinka, 'The Telephone Conversation'

There is strong evidence that eighteenth-century Britain was home to 10,000 black people. There were African-born farm workers in Norfolk and Cumbria, and the English nobility indulged an exotic passion for collecting black servants. Further back in history, the Roman fortress at Aballava, near Carlisle, was garrisoned by North African troops.

A recent report published by the Commission for Racial Equality (CRE) points out that in Cornwall, Devon, Dorset and Somerset alone the number of residents in 1981 whose country of origin was in Africa, Asia, the Caribbean or Latin America was 32,600, and argues that this figure for black and ethnic minority people resident in the four counties today, including those born in England, is not likely to have declined. A very rough calculation that there were perhaps 137,000 people from an ethnic minority background living in rural England and Wales during 1991.

Julian Agyeman, Chair of the Black Environment Network (BEN) which seeks to raise awareness of environmental issues among black and ethnic minority communities, as well as encouraging them to visit the countryside, has many views on why such groups tend to visit rural England. A recent survey by the government's countryside access advisers, the Countryside Commission, demonstrated that people from 'multi-racial areas' and those from 'the poorest council estates' were least likely to go out into the countryside.

Agyeman, an environmental educationalist, points to culture, the time and economics of 'getting out', lack of appropriate publicity and fear, as factors keeping black and ethnic minorities away from the countryside as visitors and residents. He believes that many of the original immigrants to Britain fled from rural poverty.

The city is associated with progress, the country with backwardness; with spirits and creatures that can do you harm. It is not seen as a recreational resource but as a producer of food . . . this black absence from the countryside will change with the present younger generation going on field trips at school. But this does not absolve bodies such as the Countryside Commission from their moral obligation to promote access for all by using positive imagery. Older people will go, they just need encouragement and appropriate publicity.

It is a mistake to view the rural community as a homogeneous lump. In the same way different ethnic groups come from different backgrounds and may display a variety of attitudes and characteristics. First generation Punjabi Sikhs, for example, came from middle income groups whose members emigrated, not to escape grinding poverty but to improve the economic and social positions of their families in the Punjab (by remittances which were used to buy more land). Additionally, towns and villages in the Punjab are relatively developed both in terms of agriculture and light industry. Rural Punjab for those who left – many of whom were 'de-skilled' once they arrived here, taking up jobs for which they were overqualified – was far from being a backward backwater.

Race Relations

So what are the experiences of people from an ethnic minority background, who live and work in England's countryside? First of all, it is clear that racial prejudice, in common with many areas of life, cannot be conveniently pigeonholed in terms of 'acceptance' or 'hostility'. There are degrees of tolerance. As Mr Mistry, a 38-year-old Asian village postmaster puts it, 'There are one or two odd customers, but generally we feel at home here. Mind you, our 12-year-old son has had to put up with the occasional taunts of "Paki" from schoolmates...he's the only Asian pupil out of 1,200 students. Sometimes it's hard for him.'

In 1975 Mr Mistry and his wife travelled 5,000 miles from Gujerat in India to find work. During 1988 he packed up his own business in Northampton and moved to a nearby village. 'The local community openly acknowledges that we have improved the shop and post office substantially. The previous owners were a white couple incidentally. I see myself as a public servant and villagers respond to this – we're respected and I can go where I like without feeling self-conscious.'

With only two commercial outlets, the village is obviously keen to retain its shop: 'Recently we were held up at gunpoint – they cleaned out the post office takings. But do you know, the following day we were flooded with cards from wellwishers; neighbours dropped by to say how sorry they were and we filled 15 buckets with flowers! This is an indication of how local people feel about us', says Mr Mistry. But he sounds a cautionary note,

> I have no complaints but I do know one Asian friend, in another village, whose takings have dropped by 50 per cent since he took on the business and who is now facing bankruptcy. I've heard of other shops where a black person has been forced to close down through lack of custom, and where a white successor has succeeded financially. You understand what I'm saying?

Barbara Browne lived for six and a half years in the North Yorkshire village of Brayton – until acts of vandalism, verbal and physical abuse drove her away. In this otherwise white community Barbara felt like a prisoner. 'You couldn't do anything an dthings got steadily worse. First they cut down the clothes line, then there was the fencing. Eggs were shoved through the letterbox.' Mud and excrement were also thrown through open windows. Barbara Browne felt under siege. The final straw came when granddaughter Lucinda was kicked and punched on her way home from school – local teenagers were suspected. Barbara packed up and left to stay with friends. Her story was shown on the BBC's *CountryFile* programme in August 1992. She displayed great compassion but broke down at the last: 'If I hated them then I'd be just as they are. But I wish people could understand that we're human beings too…we didn't choose our colour, race or creed. We just have to accept what we are. And they are lucky they're white.…'

Also on the programme was Mustafa Shaikh. He moved 10 years ago from Wolverhampton to Taunton in Somerset. Mustafa felt that country people are less aware of the offence they can cause. 'People here still use a language that I find totally inappropriate, referring to black people as "darkies", "coloureds" and "negroes".' He believed that many rural areas display characteristics from their colonial past – including the presumption of white supremacy.

Deborah Phillips, in research at Leeds University, has uncovered some appalling behaviour relating to race and access to the property market. "Some estate agents made openly racist remarks even though we were taping them. They tried to discourage black custom, for example by failing to send out details relating to "higher status" properties.' Although this work was urban-oriented (Bedford town), the estate agents were covering a wider area and made it clear that they wished to preserve the 'traditional' (white) character of the countryside. Estate agents associated black minorities with the inner city. Deborah Phillips went on to comment that a recent British Social Attitudes Survey had shown that one-third of white people interviewed had expressed attitudes that indicated racial prejudice. In a village of 500 people you could face 150 hostile neighbours.

The 1992 research findings from the Commission for Racial Equality give further grounds for concern. Then CRE Chairman, Sir Michael Day, points to a 'disturbing picture of racial prejudice and discrimination. While a few organisations and individuals are taking positive steps to promote racial equality, there is mostly widespread complacency – or worse – in the majority white community.'

The 'worse' is not hard to pinpoint – incidents of discrimination, violence, harassment, condescension and bigotry. Eric Jay believes that 'the problems experienced by black and ethnic minority people living in rural areas need to be seen in context, in particular that of the failure of many public authorities to implement anti-racist and equal opportunity policies'.

An opinion poll of students in the construction department of a further education college in the Southwest revealed that 35 per cent of respondents viewed 'blacks/Asians' in a negative way. The survey produced some shocking individual replies: 'They all smell of shit and wear crepe bandages on their heads', leading to the conclusion that 'they could soon be invading us . . . keep them in Birmingham'.

Julian Agyeman feels that 'many "white" people have deliberately escaped to the countryside and actively want to retain the "Arcadian dream". It's these people who have left the rush and tear of the city, including a perceived threat of racial violence and who now want to pull up the drawbridge.' He argues that a lot of 'new villagers' not only adopt NIMBY (not in my backyard) and NODAM(no development after mine) attitudes in relation to further housing, but that there is also a hardcore who believe they have left blacks behind in the city and certainly do not want to find them re-emerging in the heart of the country.

Katie Ivens, in a letter to the *Daily Telegraph* (April 1991), mischeviously poked fun at the Countryside Commission, who had been previously quoted as wanting villagers 'not to stare at blacks'. Ms Ivens retorted that 'as country people stare at all visitors surely it would be racist not to stare at black people'. This does carry the grain of truth. Julian Agyeman recounts: 'As a black man I can walk into a country pub and it's like the Wild West – the piano stops and people stare expectantly – waiting for you to swing from the rafters.' But he also goes on to explain that words and looks are only the half of it; there is also the fear of physical violence. This prompted one black American visitor and her British friend to carry concealed baseball bats with them on hiking expeditions. There is the more celebrated example of comedians, Lenny Henry and Dawn French, hounded by racists in their Berkshire village. 'We came home one night and the letters "NF" were smeared in excrement above the door.' Other fanatics left the disturbing message 'You have been visited by the Klu Klux Klan.'

> The Treatment of Minorities is a Barometer of a Society's Moral Health...
>
> *Rabbi Hugo Gryn, 'The Moral Maze', Radio 4,*
> *3 September 1992*

Jennie Merriman moved from inner-city Sheffield to become a youth worker in Derbyshire's Hope Valley. She rapidly discovered that young people, and the community in general, had never met a black person in their lives. As a result, 13 local youth workers got together 'to create opportunities for people from the Derbyshire Dales to get to know black workers and young people from other areas in an easy and positive way'. Nice idea but how did it work in practice? A 'fun weekend' was staged including music workshops, rock climbing, self-defence and tennis coaching. Through these activities white youngsters from rural Derbyshire were thrown into the company of black young people from Derby. There was no formal or overt attempt to discuss racism.

Jennie feels that 'the formula worked. The activities were tackled energetically . . . and many stayed up well into the night just chatting and mixing freely.' A second event cemented friendships and a more ambitious plot was hatched: Gwen Tresidder, one of the young women, recalls that the group 'wanted a trip to France. The youth workers said it couldn't be done. We had a meeting without them and said it could be done.' The upshot was the establishment of the Multi-Cultural Urban Rural Youth Link project (MURYL). Members met socially, developed relationships and fired the adults with their enthusiasm and energy.

This culminated in a visit to the French city of Bourg-en-Bresse, followed by a week in a remote Alpine village. The trip was an ordinary mix: worries about cliques, personality clashes and misunderstandings, and included a trip to the hospital when someone trapped their finger in the door of the minibus. But 'the group sorted things out. They learnt a lot, co-operated and strengthened friendships. This was really the secret of the whole project. People from vastly different backgrounds whom geography normally kept apart, mixed together and became close as they broke down the barriers that were assumed to come between them', concludes Jennie Merriman. Like all good community work the benefits of this project permeated well beyond those directly affected.

Jennie sums up by commenting that the difficulties encountered in this initiative 'were mainly due to the fundamental nature of rural work – the distances, the lack of transport, problems of communication and the lack of resources. But the rewards were worth it.'

Celebrating the Creativity of a Village

Chiddingly is 'in the middle of nowhere in "bush Sussex" and boasts a magnificent pile of stones – the thirteenth-century parish church – a pub, village school and shop – the social centre of the universe'. This thumbnail sketch is provided by Noel Hardy, founding chair and leading light in the remarkable Chiddingly Festival. Since 1979 this small village of 640 people has staged its own week-long 'celebration of the arts and local talent, whilst also presenting performers of international standing'. Artists from as far afield as Africa, South America and the Ukraine bring their music and dance to the Festival and share an authentic, traditional meal as part of the proceedings. Bea Gatrell, one of the organisers and born and bred in the village, emphasises that 'the musical evening in the village hall is very special, with a feeling of mixing and mingling, a sense of unity'. Through entertainment villagers have the opportunity to learn about different cultures. Although Brighton is only 20 miles away and stages its own major arts event – second only in scale to the Edinburgh Festival – Chiddingly has attracted an impressive range of contributors. James Berry, the award-winning Jamaican poet, and Guyanese poet John Agard have given readings in the Six Bells pub. During 1989 the black African Group, Shikisha (meaning 'belt it out' in Zulu), who also performed at the Live Aid Concert in London, danced and sang to thunderous approval in the local hall and led children in bead-making workshops in the village school.

Noel Hardy believes that the Chiddingly Festival – a recognised charity now in its fifteenth year – 'has achieved a unique reputation for innovation, and for bringing high quality events to an area otherwise denied them on account of cost or accessibility. We are conscious of the richness and variety of art forms from other cultures and want as many people as possible to experience them and share the benefits.'

Attitudes to Strangers

It is important to see attitudes towards race as an extreme manifestation of a more general rural conundrum – how to integrate increasing numbers of ex-urban incomers. Local authorities in East

Anglia, for example, predict the arrival of 130,000 newcomers by the year 2011 creating a need for 81,000 additional homes. Canon Anthony Russell, a commentator on rural affairs, observes that as a result of this massive migration to rural areas the modern village has become a 'community of communities comprised of groups of people who have different understandings about the nature of the village and the future of the countryside'. It is equally apparent that, as Tory MP David Heathcoat-Amory put it in a parliamentary debate in April 1990,

> Newcomers to villages are often essential. If we are worried about the fact that there are not enough people to keep the local post office open or about the village shop not having enough customers or the village school not having enough pupils, we must welcome newcomers . . . we do not want to create or preserve living museums in our rural areas.

The report *Integration of Newcomers*, produced in 1991 by the campaigning Suffolk ACRE, investigated nine local settlements and concluded that although integration was evident it could not be taken for granted:

> In some of the places we studied there appears a real divide between existing residents and newcomers. As time goes by it is often the newcomers who begin to take initiatives in the community which can lead to resentment from the older residents. The whole process could be more positive if organisations in the community got together to plan a welcome to newcomers. Existing residents should not expect newcomers to immediately join in everything. The demands of the move usually keep people housebound for some time, but the goodwill of receiving an invitation or a visit can at least lead to people beginning to know each other.

Work by Save the Children in rural Powys demonstrated that newcomers can provide the spark for local initiatives.

> By getting involved in self-help and helping others they tap into

networks of support that were otherwise unavailable to them. This can sustain them as individuals and create something worthwhile for their communities. . . . If self-help is to be effective as a means of bringing help and change to people in their own communities it needs to be supported.

'Sensitivity' and an inclination to understand people from different backgrounds must underpin the successful integration of incomers, whether they are black or white. The Church of England's review *Faith in the Countryside* (1990) goes on to say that for communal life to have any real meaning it must be founded on 'justice, corporate responsibility, protection of the disadvantaged', through neighbourliness, love, compassion and mutual care. And as Julian Agyeman concludes: 'We've concentrated for so long on urban racism – where most black people live. Myself and BEN have been pushing the rural side of racism for years and now people are beginning to take notice.'

The Myths and Realities of Rural Crime

Incest was common where the Roads were Bad

Laurie Lee

Rural areas are commonly associated with sex offences. News reports about ritual child sex abuse on Scottish islands, incest or the widespread abuse of children in care in rural Wales, fuel such speculation. Bestiality also remains a powerful rural stereotype. But as Allan Peggie, a Probation Service researcher, comments:

As far as I can see, it is a myth; worthy of note principally as a reflection of the stereotyped images which urban dwellers have of those who live in the country. What statistics appear to show – and I have had access to both Police and Probation Service sources – is that sex offences or sex offenders can appear more prevalent in rural areas because other sorts of offending are substantially less prevalent.

The same is probably true of violent offences, which tend to figure prominently in police and probation records for rural areas, and are increasingly recognised as a problem in small towns. This again does not mean that country dwellers are more violent by nature – it simply demonstrates that they commit other types of offences less often than those living in urban areas. And the main cause of violence in the country appears to be the same as it is in the cities – alcohol. Allan Peggie comments in relation to Northeast England that 'a greater proportion of offenders on probation in rural districts also have alcohol problems'.

The other dimension to rural or small town violence is that it is not necessarily committed by local people against local people. A crucial distinction needs to be drawn between crime committed in the countryside and crime committed by country dwellers.

A Question of Scale

That burglary, theft and criminal damage are not as prevalent in rural areas does not mean that villagers never commit such offences. Where it does occur as an indigenous activity it tends to be in pockets of social deprivation which, on a smaller scale, replicate the conditions found in those urban – or 'inner city' – areas in which crime rates are at their highest. Some of the former mining communities in Durham and Northumberland, for example, have particularly high rates and while juvenile delinquency is not generally a major problem in the countryside. One rurally-based Probation Officer described his cases as in the main 'more sad than bad'. According to Inspector Greg Lawrence of the West Mercia Force, 'Drug and solvent abuse can take hold in small communities and lead to other forms of offending while alcohol abuse among the young in particular can be a problem. The pub is often the only youth club and can be the source of much local crime.' The same range of offences is committed in rural locations and for the same reasons as in urban areas, but in different proportions.

Distinctive Features

Certain aspects of rural life do have an impact on crime – on how much is reported, on its victims and offenders.

The physical isolation of some country dwellers has a bearing on crime in a number of ways. Conventional crime prevention hinges on the idea that criminals are not deterred by security measures, however sophisticated, if the prospect of detention and arrest are slight. In some parts of the countryside, where homes or groups of properties are left empty for substantial parts of the day, where police patrols are infrequent or non-existent and where the police response to reported incidents is necessarily slow, there can be little defence against break-ins. As one respondent put it when asked why she did not have a burglar alarm: 'Well there isn't much the sheep could do about it if it went off.'

Isolation also magnifies the fear of crime, particularly among those who have already become its victims. This is a challenge to police and victim support schemes operating in rural areas. And, as in the case of services catering for those with health or social welfare problems, wide catchment areas and poor public transport mean that facilities for both offenders and victims are necessarily constrained, although no less innovative than those found in the cities.

While physical isolation has an effect on crime, so too does the social closeness of some rural communities. Police sources confirm the suspected under-reporting of rural crime because of the need to minimise discord or conflict within such communities. Farmers, according to one officer, can make life difficult so, for example, illegal methods used by landowners to control wildlife persist. And although those involved in badger-baiting may well be known, convictions are infrequent because potential informants know that they too can easily be identified.

According to victim support – a voluntary network – problems resulting from being on the receiving end of crime are more difficult to address where the victim and perpetrator are known to each other and to most other members of the community, each of whom will have formed their own views concerning blame. This is particularly true for women victims of violence or sex offences, who can still experience a high degree of stigma from rural residents. And help for victims can be difficult to obtain. In an article published in *The Independent* in 1988, Sarah Nelson drew attention to the plight of 'battered wives' on the Outer Hebrides:

> Try travelling for help to Stornoway, try walking miles to a phone to find it has been vandalised, or escaping by ferry in bad weather, or when everything stops on Sunday.
>
> How do you seek confidential help when the postman sees all your envelopes, or run away with the children when your husband is at home working on the croft? Dare you confide in the social worker or doctor when everyone knows everyone else, when word might get back to your husband?

Rural victims, in other words, can find it less easy to distance themselves from the crimes committed against them than those in urban areas. The same is true for the perpetrators. It is a feature of small communities that most, if not all, crime is reported in the local press. The local community will not only be aware of what the offender has done but also what sentence has been imposed. The result is that rehabilitation too – whether through probation, community service or supervision following release from prison – will take place under a knowing public gaze. A reputation once acquired can be difficult to shake off; families as well as individuals can be tarnished in this way. Cities have 'bad areas', small towns their 'bad ends' but in the country 'bad families', as judged by the community, are the highly personalised focus of stereotypes about crime.

While this picture may persist in the more traditional or remoter rural areas, Inspector Greg Lawrence in Worcester puts a different perspective on crime in the more accessible countryside: 'Criminals bank on two things; the first is anonymity and the second is a breakdown in community cohesion, so that self-regulation or disciplining is no longer exercised. In many country areas the 'checks and balances' of social control are evaporating.'

City Criminals Come to the Country

Not all violence or – it could be added – public order offences are committed by rural inhabitants against other country residents. Rural 'disturbances' have resulted from skirmishes between residents and 'outsiders' or, on a larger scale, there have been 'invasions' of the countryside by New Age Travellers, accompanied by subsequent clashes with police and local people. On Hereford and Worcester's Castle Morton Common, for example, around 25,000 people congregated during the summer of 1992. Such happenings have been seasonal and relatively infrequent, but with an undoubted effect.

Perhaps the most visible sign of increasing, imported, crime can be seen in the notices found at many beauty spots, warning visitors about car thefts. This, together with more burglaries, armed robbery and ram raids, though not at levels found in urban areas, demonstrates that rural areas are within the reach of city-based criminals.

The urban-to-rural displacement of crime has three elements. First is the spread of preventative measures in urban areas such as increased security and surveillance. This has led urban criminals to look for new 'softer' targets. The second factor is that rural areas have many such targets and this is not just because rural properties are more vulnerable by virtue of their isolation. It also results from the attitude of rural dwellers towards security. It seems only recently that country residents have begun to acknowledge, reluctantly, that premises and vehicles should always be kept secure. The third factor, which links the other two, is that criminals are highly mobile, in part the result of a growing pool of experienced and competent car thieves.

The long-term effects of urban-based criminals penetrating the countryside are not clear. Their activities could result in the development of a siege mentality, increasing mistrust of outsiders among longstanding rural residents or the use of illegal means of protection.

Allan Peggie concludes that 'rural crime cannot be viewed in isolation from other social and economic developments now overtaking the countryside, and from the changing relationship between town and country. Crime must not be treated as an exclusively urban phenomenon.'

Chapter 4

Housing and Homelessness

A place in the country – everyone's ideal.
Bryan Ferry/Roxy Music

Black and white images flicker on a screen; this is the 1940s film of C.S. Orwin's study into *40 Square Miles* of North Oxfordshire (with a youthful John Arlott as commentator). Scenes from a bygone era – yet within living memory – show how poor and squalid many country houses were with primitive outside toilets, cramped, overcrowded and doubtful conditions for food preparation and storage, inconvenient, ineffective and dirty coal fires. You might well think that these early problems are now dead and that the real – and only – housing issue in rural England relates to affordability.

Help the Aged has recently published a report by Daniel Pearson on the housing conditions of older people in rural areas. He concluded that 'elderly people in rural areas occupy some of the worst housing and that the poor condition of a large proportion of the private rented stock, in which a large number of people over the age of 75 live, makes them particularly vulnerable'. This is confirmed by the *English House Condition Survey*, published in 1988, which makes sober reading. The proportion of dwellings in poor condition was 22 per cent in the countryside, compared with only 14 per cent for urban areas, owner occupiers in rural locations were one and a half times more likely to live in poor housing and 48 per cent of private rented properties were in a bad state in comparison with 40 per cent in the cities. Here are three shocks: (i) that the fabric of many rural houses remains so poor; (ii) that conditions are worse in the country than the town; and (iii) that in spite of the statistics the perception remains of inner city decay and rural affluence. From a survey carried out during 1989, Daniel Pearson observed that substandard houses and those lacking basic amenities are 'particularly concentrated in rural areas, with the 100 most rural shire districts having a greater share of unfit housing than the 97 most urban, including cities such as Bristol, Middlesbrough, Leicester and Nottingham'.

In 1991 the Royal Colleges of Physicians of the UK published a report on *Housing or Homelessness: A Public Health Perspective.* This study commented that the 'relationship between ill health, poor housing standards and sanitation has long been established and indeed constituted the basis for the original housing legislation of the nineteenth century'. It is a sad indictment to find that the adverse influence of poor housing 'on physical and mental health and on social well-being is undoubtedly real' as we near the millennium.

The National Children's Home (NCH) investigated the link between poverty and nutrition during 1991. One in five parents questioned

> said they had gone hungry in the last month, December 1990, because they did not have enough money to buy food . . . poor diet was directly correlated with food expenditure. The survey showed that there was no evidence to suggest that parents are ignorant about what constitutes a healthy diet. They were unable to provide themselves or their families with an adequate diet because of their income.

Specifically in a rural context, and as an additional burden, the NCH work highlighted the fact that 'in rural and inner city areas, the cost of buying healthy foods was consistently higher'.

So we can pinpont the origin of a vicious circle: poverty leading to poor housing and diet, producing mental and other illness,

An elderly man outside his home, an example of
unfit housing in rural Devon
(James Ravilious, Beaford Archive)

particularly among the elderly. Brian McLaughlin's 1986 *Rural Deprivation Study* 'found that a quarter of all households in the rural survey were living in poverty or on the margins of poverty as defined by state standards of eligibility for supplementary benefit and associated payments . . . the problem of poverty is heavily but not exclusively concentrated among the elderly. . . .'

On p. 84 Posy Simmonds casts a wry look at rural housing then . . . and now.

Staying Put – In Eden

Eden District council and Anchor Housing have embarked on a pioneering project in rural Cumbria. Almost one in five of the district population is of pensionable age. 'Staying Put aims to keep elderly people independent and in their own homes. It provides a helping hand through the maze of potential grants on offer. And for the local authority there is a direct cost-saving on OAP or sheltered

Old Arcadia/New Arcadia (© Posy Simmonds)

accommodation that would otherwise have to be built', argues Paul Mardell, the project co-ordinator.

The Staying Put initiative is a fully kitted-out van, Paul, and back-up from Eden's environmental health, planning and other staff.

> We have two aims: first to reach householders who through personal circumstances or geography have no effective access to advice on home improvements. Second, to provide an 'all-in-one' service, so that we take the strain of co-ordinating and negotiating with the architect, council departments, builders, building society, bank and others who have a stake in home improvements. It's my job to make it all happen. The elderly client deals only with me, while I juggle the various players to make sure the work is done.

Since the start of the project, March 1990, and September 1992 91 houses have been improved at a total cost of £493,698. The majority, £444,990, has been recouped in the form of housing grants from central government. Andrew Yates in Eden's technical services department observes that 'the use of a mobile office to visit clients in outlying areas and the ability to operate on the move was something that we had never tried before. The Council and Anchor can feel proud that with vision and co-operation we have produced a model in the housing agency field.'

Paul Mardell adds 'The main advantage of the van is that it advertises the service wherever it goes. I can be reached by mobile phone so if I'm in a particular vicinity and a call to visit comes in unexpectedly, I have the chance to work this into my schedule without the waste of time and extra mileage of returning to Penrith first.' The local authority is convinced that a static office would not be as effective – the rent plus company car and mileage from the town to isolated clients would be costly, wasteful and less efficient.

Paul has a potential clientele of 8,900 elderly and disabled people out of the District's 46,000 population.

> 80–90 per cent of callers are entitled to state benefits (usually council tax relief). This automatically makes them eligible for a range of home improvement grants, which also cover an additional administration cost. We can reduce or waive the project fee where clients are unable to afford this. There are incidental benefits from visiting people in their own homes – I can make referrals to occupational therapists, Age Concern and individual local authority departments, to secure benefits other than straightforward home improvements. It's an all round service.

Good relations between Staying Put and other district council officers have been crucial to the success of the project. Eden has decided to provide discretionary minor works grants of up to £1,000 a time. This is for simple, but important, things like fitting new doors to make a house weatherproof.

Paul Mardell comments that 'it costs about £33,000 a year to keep the service running; this covers depreciation on the van, salary, petrol, telephone, postage and so on'. In 30 months Paul has covered 44,600 miles. The project officer averages two calls per day – many of which can be pretty involved!

Anchor employs the co-ordinator but he works hand-in-glove with local authority staff. Elderly clients gain peace of mind from an independent, single point of contact with all the players that have a practical say in home improvements. Central government can be sure that its grants are being effectively targeted and efficiently spent. The district council is able to serve a disadvantaged segment of its electorate and save considerable sums through improving existing houses rather than having to custom-build new ones. And Anchor, a housing association, receives excellent publicity and is well placed for future low-cost housing ventures in the area.

The Department of Environment will fund 50 per cent of the project for five years up to 1995 so the degree of risk for the district council is limited. The van was donated by the Monument Charitable Trust.

Paul Mardell concludes by saying that

Eden has decided to establish an in-house agency, to provide a more comprehensive service to grant applicants, which the project will also be able to take advantage of. This should overcome the main obstacle that we currently face – delays caused by building firms failing to do their work on time. Other than that, we're 'Staying Put'.

Affordable Rural Housing

The richest crop for any field
Is a crop of bricks for it to yield.
The richest crop that it can grow
Is a crop of houses in a row.

A Rhyme from the 1830s

Lord Shuttleworth, Chairman of the Rural Development Commission, acknowledges that 'more and more people simply cannot afford anywhere to live in the countryside'. The RDC recommends urgent action by government. Local authorities, severely constrained by the Treasury in terms of public expenditure, should be able to re-invest more than the current 25 per cent of income generated by the sale of council houses to help build new homes. Researchers from Bristol University also suggest that 'suitable land and property in rural areas owned by public authorities – such as the Ministry of Defence – should be released to boost the supply of affordable homes through local authorities or housing associations'.

The community council for Hertfordshire, a local voluntary organisation, describes the problem:

> In the last decade it has become increasingly difficult for local people with modest incomes to acquire a dwelling in their home village. The causes are many. Economic prosperity and increased mobility for some have enabled those who are attracted to the idea of country living to compete for housing.... In addition increased longevity and smaller, but more numerous, households have often resulted in a mismatch between the type and size of houses needed and those that are available. The rural housing problem has been exacerbated by the continual decrease of privately let accommodation at reasonable rents, the sale of council houses as well as the loss of tied accommodation. Financial restrictions on District Councils limit their ability to provide new housing direct.

Although state-subsidised schemes are not the be-all and end-all of rural housing supply, they do illustrate the growing chasm between need and response. The government's Housing Corporation aims to provide funding for just 6,460 rural houses in the three-year period 1992–5. Since the 'Right to Buy' legislation was introduced in 1980 more than 95,000 council houses were bought in the period to March 1991 in the 63 'predominantly rural districts' – those areas used as a barometer for change in England's countryside. This amounts to three out of ten rural council houses (33 per cent) sold into private hands – well above the national average of 25 per cent. Only one new house was built by local authorities and housing associations for every three council houses discarded. This amounts to a loss of 20 per cent of the public housing stock between 1980 and 1991. During 1992 district planning officers identified sections of society which have 'become increasingly disadvantaged as a result of these trends: young couples on average or below average incomes, the elderly whose present accommodation is no longer suitable but for whom no alternative exists. . . .' And these vulnerable groups, even if they are fortunate enough to be offered a housing association property, can expect to pay £70 maximum per week in rent. The ACRE/Rural Development Commission 1992 survey of *Rural Social Housing* expressed 'new fears about affordability as association rents move towards economic rents and mean that only those entitled to full housing benefit are likely to be housed by associations'. Diana Farrow of the Wiltshire Rural Housing Association confirms that many of her tenants are fearful of taking on poorly paid rural jobs because, with a potential pay packet of around £90 a week, 'they will find themselves worse off than if they'd stayed unemployed and entitled to full benefits'.

Steve Wilcox, a housing specialist at the University of Wales, goes on to suggest that '100,000 borrowers in 1992, in mortgage arrears (one-fifth of the total), are working for the sake of working and would indeed be far better off on the dole'. So what action is being taken to redress the acute shortage of affordable housing? A crucial element in the provision of new homes is the price of land.

Benevolent Landowners

In February 1989 Michael Howard, then Minister for Planning, accepted that planning permission could be granted for 'affordable' housing on sites which would not normally gain consent, and where there was a demonstrable need. the Royal Town Planning Institute (RTPI) commented that this represented 'a use of the planning system to subsidise the provision of low-cost housing through containment of land value which is critical to the provision of dwellings at affordable prices/rents'. But there are problems in this approach. First there is the 'lottery factor', dependence on locating a willing vendor. Then there is the danger that any land offered will be the least acceptable in planning terms and the most costly to develop.

Local authorities commonly employ 'Section 106' agreements to restrict occupancy on a plot of land to local people in housing need. Restrictive covenants, applied by the landowner, are another way of determining what use can be made of a particular site. However price and tenure are not directly controlled by these mechanisms and it is therefore important to work with organisations who are committed to the principle of affordable housing.

More worrying is the statement by the District Planning Officers' Society that benevolent landowners could only deliver 'a token contribution to the supply of new affordable housing'.

Land Banks

From Devon and Northumberland come two glimmers of hope. In both cases Community Councils have launched 'Land Banks'. Dr David Francis, Director of the Northumberland Council, explains: 'We are asking owners to offer small plots of land at low or no cost. The Land Bank will not buy the land but take out a five year option.' This will allow time to find a suitable developer, from the public or private sector, enable funds to be raised and negotiation of binding agreements so that the houses built will be both low-cost and available only to local people in perpetuity. Obtaining land at less than its full market value increases the chance of houses being within the price range of local people. The Land Bank is overseen by a small group of highly influential people, including a land agent and chartered surveyor, retired chief executive and planning officer from the county council and a landowner who used to head the Country Landowners' Association (CLA) in the Northeast.

The Devon Land Bank was the first in the country and Gayle Kirrage, a community development worker with the scheme, explains its operation: 'We provide a trustworthy shelter for the philanthropic landowner. The Land Bank has the effect of calming the fears of planners and landowners, that any new development really will benefit local people and will have a 'cast iron' legal framework to ensure this.' Grant aid of £8,700 to establish the Land

Bank Trust came from the Dartmoor National Park Authority and Rural Development Commission. By mid 1992 22 houses had been financed and built through the Devon Land Bank. These were in the small mid-Devon village of Sandford and at Budleigh Salterton (East Devon). Of these 17 were built for rent, with the remainder on a part-mortgage/part-rent basis (shared equity).

Ian Scott, who reviewed the Devon scheme in 1992, concluded that it is making

> a practical contribution to one aspect of the current rural housing crisis, the high cost of sites, and the consequent forcing of people away from their home village due to the lack of affordable housing. Having said that, it has proved a complicated, and at times slow, process to move forward the idea to the actual provision of homes for local occupation.

In 1993/4 £820,000 (enough to finance around 30 homes) has been earmarked to be spent by housing associations via the Land Bank; this could revolutionise its operation.

The Archbishops of Canterbury and York's Commission on Rural Areas recommended that the Church 'as owners of glebe and investment land, should take a lead in showing the responsibilities of landowners towards rural housing provision. They should invite district housing officers to inspect the register of Church land holdings to enable land suitable for affordable housing to be identified.' In 1992 the Rural Development Commission launched a new grant scheme for agencies 'who wish to operate a system of securing suitable sites for affordable housing'.

Land Banks take time to deliver small-scale solutions to local problems. They are part of the treatment and not a cure for the current housing 'sickness'.

Converted Farm Buildings

In England planning permission has been given for around 70,000 farmhouses and cottages since 1947, in locations where consent would normally have been refused. Farmers have argued that they needed these properties to house farm staff, for example those working unsociable hours. Already Ashford Council in Kent is pioneering a new policy, allowing single farm dwellings on the edge of villages to be occupied by local people in housing need. Consultant, David Clark, takes this idea a step further and argues that

> it would make sense, where possible, to deal with existing properties in the same way as new houses. It could be agreed that, where the existing occupancy condition is not appropriate, there could be some relaxation to provide for a broader link with the rural economy. This should be tied in to a shared ownership deal in which the existing owner would sell equity equivalent to the build cost with the difference vested in a bona fide housing association, with the usual long-term controls.

Cross-subsidy

A 1990 report, *Involving the Private Sector in Rural Housing*, argued that

> acceptance of the concept of cross-subsidy may be controversial. Members and officers of planning authorities may prefer to give planning consent on sites outside the village envelope to schemes where 100 per cent of the houses are made available to people on moderate incomes. But the sale of some houses to subsidise the production costs of the rest opens up many opportunities which will otherwise be lost.

Unfortunately Government Planning Policy Guidance (no. 3, March 1992) expressed the view that cross-subsidy was unacceptable for 'off plan' sites in rural areas. The Royal Town Planning Institute (RTPI) has addressed this same issue from another perspective; the RTPI advocates that 'local planning authorities should be allowed to adopt quota policies specifying the proportion of housing within schemes above a given size threshold (e.g. 2 hectares or 50 dwellings) that can be required to be social (i.e. rented or shared equity)'.

These different approaches represent creative thinking in 'making the best of a bad job'. But one district council chief executive spoke for many when he said 'if we were able to spend a fraction of the money generated by council house sales, the rural housing problem could be solved overnight'. The government's November 1992 Autumn Statement opened up the possibility of local authorities spending their capital receipts, over a limited period, on further house building. But Catherine Chater, ACRE's housing adviser, questioned at the time 'whether a significant level of revenue can be generated between now and December 1993 and whether local authorities will choose to spend this money on rural housing'. The Housing Corporation's 1991/2 *Annual Report* stresses that 'the level of housing need in rural areas is one of the hidden problems facing British housing'.

Down and Out in Rural England

Sarah Lawrenson talked quietly about her impending homelessness.

> We moved into the small Cotswold village of Chedworth expecting to rent for three years. After just a single year our landlord unexpectedly returned from overseas. We love the house, the community, and my 10-year-old son is settled at the local school – but we've had to move out and the prospect of finding somewhere else is uncertain.

Sarah's plight isn't just an isolated case of bad luck – she's one of 14,000 country people who don't have a regular roof over their head. Of those registered as 'homeless' in England 14 per cent live in rural areas. Life can be particularly hard for young, single, homeless people.

> Young Ladies Who Get Pregnant Just to Jump the Housing List ...
>
> *Peter Lilley, Secretary of State for Social Security, 1992*

Rachel, who was 18 and studying 'A' levels at a college of arts and technology in the North of England, left home following the breakdown of her relationship with parents.

I packed my case and went out of the house. As soon as I was on the doorstep I felt degraded and embarrassed – embarrassed at walking along the road with a big suitcase; I felt everyone was looking and talking about me. I didn't know where I was going. A friend's mother put me up for the night. At that time people generally wouldn't help because they knew my parents and didn't want to get involved.

I went to the housing department to register as homeless. They said I wasn't a priority case. I signed on the council house waiting list and was told that they would consider me in a year's time. At the Department of Social Security (DSS) I found that I was not eligible for benefit because I was registered for a grant – my tuition fees were paid but I received no grant because my parents earned too much.

I had no choice but to leave college because I had no money for the travel there and back. After daily visits to the DSS for three weeks, they finally agreed to give me income support – £32 a week. I stayed at my friend's for two weeks but had to leave because I just couldn't afford the £30 a week board she was asking. Another friend's mother offered to put me up for £10 a week so I went there. I then got a training post, and was able to pay £15 rent. Eight months later I am still here. I often feel that I shouldn't be, because there are five other adults and me and four children aged 17, 16, 5 and 2 in a four-bedroomed house. But they don't seem to mind and I am very grateful for them putting me up, otherwise I don't know what I'd have done.

I have tried to find somewhere else to live – I had hopes of a bedsit in the local market town, but it was given to someone who was working full-time. I have got very little prospect of getting anywhere. People tell me I should get pregnant and have a baby, then I would be housed – but I want to finish my training and get a job. I want to be independent.

John was in his early twenties when he became homeless. His parents had divorced and had new relationships and there was no longer room for him. He was determined to stay in the area, registered as homeless and put his name on the council's waiting list. As with Rachel, he was told that his application would be considered a year hence. He spent time sleeping on friends' floors but eventually found himself with nowhere to go. For about 18 months he was forced to sleep rough. By this time he felt that he just couldn't cope with another winter outside so he moved in with a family on a temporary basis. He now lives in a flat on Tyneside – at least 40 minutes by train from his friends. City life is a far cry from his own small town roots.

Barry arrived from Telford hoping to improve his prospects and find lodgings in the historic market town of Hexham, Northumberland. Fortunately it was summer and the weather was warm – there were no lodgings so he had to sleep in the open for a couple of weeks before he was able to afford a tent. He then became involved in running a community furniture store in the town, providing equipment for other displaced people, and was able to sleep in a small caravan at the store site. Now there are plans to develop the furniture store. The caravan will lose its plot and, once again, he is faced with the prospect of nowhere to live.

A report published by the RDC in 1992 revealed that in the last four years 'the incidence of homelessness tripled in deep rural areas, and overall, rural homelessness increased at a faster rate than urban homelessness'. Cardboard City has come to Ambridge.

ACRE contributed to the material on which the *Homelessness* report is based. Catherine Chater talked grimly about 'young single people or childless couples who are being forced to leave their rural communities in search of urban shelter. These people are "rural refugees".' But why are an increasing number of people becoming homeless in England's countryside? 'Homelessness in rural areas is clearly associated with problems of affordability and high house prices. This has a direct effect (inability to buy) and an indirect effect (persuading landlords to sell property)', according to Christine

Lambert from the Bristol-based research team that completed the RDC study. In the Lincolnshire district of West Lindsey another problem is apparent. The town of Gainsborough (population 18,500) accounts for around 25 per cent of the district population; by contrast it contains almost half the entire stock of council housing. In addition to this concentration of public housing in one town has come the 'double whammy' of 1,281 properties sold from district council to private ownership under the 'right to buy' provisions of the 1980 Housing Act. A 1985 survey of Lincolnshire villages showed that in West Lindsey alone, 20 per cent had no private houses at all for rent.

David Clark points to perhaps '377,000 households requiring housing within five years. Taking a whole host of measures into account, there is still going to be a deficit of at least 120,000

Evicted from their council home for rent arrears, the Ottaway family
live in their rusting Ford Escort in their local town, East Dereham, Norfolk
(Sturrock, Network)

households for whom additional housing will be required over the five years.' Northumberland County Council has recently unearthed another contributing factor to homelessness – low pay. Chris Taylor, of the Northern Region Low Pay Unit, discovered that 'over 57 per cent of the county's employees earn below the European Decency Threshold. This amounts to over 53,600 workers. Furthermore, three out of four working women in Northumberland can be classed as low paid.' Rural incomes tend to be well below the national average while 'country homes' are increasingly sought after.

Homelessness exposes young people to illness, crime and prostitution. The London night shelter, Centrepoint, who have conducted research into rural homelessness, found in 1991 that a third of its young residents had been approached to become prostitutes since arriving in the capital. An Edinburgh-based organisation, Scottish Child, believes that the young and homeless are being victimised because they are misunderstood. Its 1991 report, *Homeless Voices*, observes: 'Leaving their parents' home is not an easy step for teenagers to take. It is often a courageous, difficult and healthy move. But a widespread belief still persists that young people leave home for frivolous reasons, and that only a few are escaping from violence or abuse.' The police response has been harsh, with 1,426 young people prosecuted during 1990 under the 1824 Vagrancy Act, which fell into disuse during the nineteenth century.

Eleanor Button, of the Centrepoint Soho Charity, goes on to point out that '60 per cent of those using the hostels and facilities in London come from outside the area. There's a national crisis in housing to be solved at a local level.' Yet another example of the way in which rural and urban areas are inextricably linked. So what is the response to rural homelessness?

Vital Links for Young Homeless

Links Youth Project in Hexham has become a local focus for young people needing help with housing. Workers and volunteers accommodate people overnight and have built up contacts with those willing to help. As a result, the project is often approached by social services for assistance in placing young people in acommodation. Links is run by a voluntary committee made up of concerned individuals and representatives from agencies such as the probation service and Council of Churches. The project depends on donations, and modest funding from the county and district councils.

Links has highlighted two problems – not only is there no emergency accommodation but neither is there any accommodation to move on to. Those who house young people on a temporary basis often find that it becomes a permanent arrangement.

This growing awareness led to the formation of a multi-agency housing group attached to Links. Over the past four years, this has sought greater recognition for the housing needs of young people in Tynedale district. It has helped young people to apply for housing and offered practical support with bedding, food and other essentials. The project has a supply of duvets to give away, so that if young people have to sleep out, they can at least keep reasonably warm.

Mike Akhurst, who is disabled, unemployed and a volunteer, runs the Links Community Furniture Store. 'It started running two days a week. Now it's more or less going over the seven days. The demand's increased a lot in the last few months. It's not just Hexham, it's the whole surrounding area.' This 'Robin Hood' service delivers beds, cookers and other household items to outlying villages and runs on donations made according to means. Mick adds that people 'are very grateful when they've got nothing and you can find something they need'.

During 1991, they conducted a survey, determining the need for single bedroom accommodation in the Hexham area. Having established this, Links secured funding from the government's Housing Corporation and identified land on which the Nomad Housing Association is building 20 single-bedroom flats. This scheme will include a unit to cover emergencies.

The Links Group has also attracted funding to appoint a housing development worker to work with young people who are homeless or at risk of becoming so. The worker will develop and encourage educational work in schools and clubs around the issues of leaving home and homelessness, will offer advice and support to young people, support them in tenancies, continue to campaign and to work more closely with the local authority in its efforts to provide adequate housing for young people.

Chapter 5

Health and Community Care

. . . there is still one commonly held myth – that there can be no ill-health associated with the countryside, as it is such an attractive place in which to live and work, and contains fewer of the hazards (poor housing, damp conditions, stress, pollution and a 'poor' environment) associated with the inner-city.

ACRE report, *Health Care in Rural England*, 1992

Dr John Derounian is one of only 280 General Practitioners (GPs) in the UK whose patient list is so small that their salary has to be topped-up to an agreed minimum. The local Health Board has agreed that GP cover is essential in this remote part of the Scottish Highlands. He is a sole practitioner with 600 patients employed mainly in the distilleries – Glenlivet and Glenfiddich – and in agriculture. 'I have to provide 24-hour cover across 280 square miles. Most of my patients live in hamlets and the largest identifiable community has a population of just 60. There are no village halls to accommodate branch surgeries.'

Dr Derounian has coined the GIG (Grass is Greener) syndrome, to describe how people settle in the area, only to leave within a short time. 'Around half of those who move in are gone after eighteen months. Visiting is one thing but experiencing the harshness of a winter up here, the awkwardness of getting about, that's what drives people away', argues Dr Derounian. He also counters the myth of rural well-being. The distilleries and farms produce their own particular difficulties. Alcohol abuse is not uncommon and ranges across excessive socialising, through progressive destruction of individual personality and home life, to the end-point – cirrhosis of the liver and death.

Among farmers, illnesses come under three categories. First there are occupational hazards, usually caused by agricultural machinery. John recalls an occasion when he was 'called out to an 18-year-old farm manager who had lost all the fingers of one hand in a "combine". Once I'd staunched the bleeding, he had an 80-mile round trip to Aberdeen, for specialist treatment.' Then there are the toxic effects of farm chemicals. 'The problem is that although a bottle may say "wear gloves when using", for a shepherd half way up a mountain, faced with a load of sheep to dip and no gloves to hand, the temptation is to ignore safety and go for convenience.' Heavy metal poisoning through skin absorption or inhalation of toxic fumes can produce liver, heart or kidney complaints. Finally, there are farm-related infections, for example Orf, viral blisters passed from lambs to humans. 'Lyme Disease' is another 'rural sickness' on the increase. Sheep ticks transmit a bacterium, related to that causing syphilis, which produces general debilitation, muscle pain or even palsy.

In 1991 Save the Children Fund queried why one Welsh Health Authority employed a vet. 'We were told that Hyatid disease is endemic in the sheep population and also the human population in South Powys.' Other effects on human health, such as miscarriage, were related to 'animal borne diseases such as campylobacter, ringworm and leptospirosis common to farming communities'.

Dr Derounian points to other challenges inherent in the job:

You have to be a general specialist! Because of the distance to the nearest casualty, I have to do all minor surgery; so for example when someone at the distillery crushed the end of a finger in a three-ton metal door, it was up to me to anaesthetise, operate and provide the after care.

Obstetrics is another responsibility. In the last year I've had to deliver three babies single-handed. In one case a woman was expecting her fourth child and between call out and arrival a few minutes later, the baby was part delivered but stuck. Eventually I pulled out an 11-pound baby but this necessitated fracturing the baby's collarbone – without immediate, drastic action both mother and child could have died.

Dr Derounian resents the administrative burdens placed upon him by the new GP contract which he feels is 'greatly interfering with the clinical side of medicine. I have to keep the records up-to-date, write all the prescriptions, do some of my own typing and monitor the business finances. There's really no let up.'

Evidence of Rural Ill-health

It's not easy to pinpoint hard evidence about the degree of poor health in rural areas. But Dr Richard Reading, a senior registrar in community paediatrics, has made urban–rural comparisons of child health based on height, birth weight, immunisation status and the coverage of screening tests. The first two are widely accepted indicators of health in childhood, while the other two are measures of the equitable provision of services. This research was carried out in Northumberland – in 1990 England's most sparsely populated county. Dr Reading concluded that 'inequalities are present in both urban and rural settings. Interestingly the differences in height between the most affluent and poorest in both urban and rural areas are greater than the average difference between urban and rural areas.'

Women, Farming and Despair

During 1989 the Women's Farm and Garden Association – founded in the nineteenth century – completed a survey on the spouses' contribution to family farm businesses. The 1,100 respondents averaged a 28-hour week of manual and clerical work; they also helped with farm policy formulation. On this basis, wives account for around 10 per cent of the regular labour input on UK farms. Dr Ruth Gasson, author of the *Hidden Workforce* survey feels that the study highlighted a number of negative features for women engaged in agriculture. 'Ten years ago, in a similar piece of research, farmers' wives stressed how much they loved the life; but this time there was much more bitterness and a general feeling of exploitation both from within the family and by society as a whole.'

More than half the women in the sample were partners in the family business but the rest had no legal status or security at all; one-third received no payment whatsoever for their contribution to the farm business. Undervalued, underpaid, overworked and often in charge of accounts which show a plummeting profit margin, it is unsurprising that farmers' wives are feeling the strain. The prices farmers could command for their produce fell by one-third in real terms during the 1980s, and average farm income has dropped to £11,000 – a 21 per cent reduction in real terms in less than a decade. It should also be remembered, as Mike Winter at the Royal Agricultural College points out, that perhaps as many as 10,000 women are farmers in their own right.

A Save the Children study, 'Swings and Roundabouts', of pre-school children and their families in rural Powys confirmed, in 1991, that mothers in the more rural parts of two study areas were more likely than those in the towns, to feel isolation and to say they needed more contact with others. One voluntary sector worker summed up the feelings of many:

> Until you've lived in a rural area it is very hard to appreciate how much it rubs off onto everything. Lack of access to information (the nearest decent library for me is 20 miles away), lack of transport times to fit in with other commitments, lack of choices and scope. These can all be got around but only with energy and effort. That is not appreciated by those in an urban setting.

In 1980 the World Health Organisation (WHO) issued a six-point strategy intended to lead to health for all by the year 2000. This commitment implies equity so that 'present inequalities in health between countries and within countries should be reduced as far as possible'. Rural people experience a range of physical and mental illness. What is the response from the relevant public and voluntary agencies?

Health Care in Rural England

A review of *English Village Services in the Eighties* painted a complex picture of provision: for example, in 1990 there were 70 more communities with a chemist than was the case in 1982. This is a direct result of the Government's rural dispensing system which has effectively provided a guaranteed income to chemists in remoter areas. Looking at the number of rural GPs, it looks very good at first sight – 13 per cent more doctors in the countryside and, generally, much more modern provision.

In 1991 the Derbyshire Family Health Services Authority (FHSA) examined the effectiveness of branch surgeries, as a decentralised service to a dispersed population, in maintaining patients' access to health care. In Derbyshire 41 per cent of practices ran branch surgeries in comparison with a national figure of 40 per cent. 'A survey involving personal interviews with 325 patients revealed high levels of patient satisfaction with services offered by branch surgeries, the elderly exhibiting higher levels of satisfaction than younger age groups.' Discussions with the GPs produced a much less sanguine view: branch surgeries had only limited opening hours, some were 'basic' in terms of equipment and comfort, but they were 'valued points of contact between the GP and less mobile patients who live in outlying settlements.... As one GP noted, "It's a question of balance. Economic viability versus social desirability."'

In England, list sizes have dropped from an average of 2,259 in 1976 to just under 2,000 in 1986. More family practitioners are dispensing their own drugs too. But such figures can be deceptive. The number of practices has fallen as family doctors have centralised in group practices; they may well be less inclined to continue branch surgeries and carry out home visits.

In 1992 Rural Voice, an alliance of 10 national countryside

bodies, argued that it was still too early to determine whether NHS and community care reforms would benefit or disadvantage rural areas. 'Greater choice of GP, quicker referrals to hospital consultants for elective surgery, more local clinics and health checks, individual case management and purchase of services could all help.' But Rural Voice raised two central issues: the first relates to choice. 'For most rural people, choice is defined by walking distance when healthy (or ill), and by the use of a car when illness, or inclination, or weather makes walking uncomfortable or impossible. This particular choice imposes costs on the user, and such costs are rarely transferred to the service provider. The National Council for Voluntary Organisations (NCVO) advanced the case for a rural premium during 1990, to account for extra costs of delivering various rural services and particularly for 'community care' which focuses on the specific needs of individuals.

The General Manager of South Lincolnshire District Health Authority acknowledged that some small rural hospitals were casualties of tough budgetary decisions forced on health authorities. He argued that regional health authorities should not adhere 'rigidly to a national formula which does not include any allowance for the added cost of solutions to problems posed by distance'.

Sussex Rural Community Council contends that changes to the NHS are 'essentially based on urban reforms designed to improve efficiency through competitive forces. These forces build on other professional areas that increasingly force medicine to be operated on a large scale.'

The Director of Public Health at Trent Regional Health Authority agreed in 1991 that authorities should try to instigate partnerships, so that services can be reinforced, and difficulties of access ameliorated. At a local level the need for an organisational, planning and management structure built around the concept of collaboration was emphasised. Dr Alderslade went on to advocate a 'seamless' pattern of care, once a patient returns to their community. 'They should not have too many people coming through their front door delivering disjointed, disorganised care. Partnership in the delivery of this care presents a management challenge for both health and social services.' In rural areas this constitutes a juggling act of immense proportions.

Community Care in Rural Areas

Perhaps the most debilitating aspect... is the difficulty of having problems taken seriously by an audience dazzled by the physical splendour, tea rooms and picture postcards.

Derwent Rural Counselling Service, 1991

The general impression is first, that people in villages have no problems, and then, if they do that they look after their own. Research by the Volunteer Centre UK in 1991 looked at the involvement of volunteers in rural areas of England. This concluded that although there was voluntary activity it was 'struggling with costs of transport and an ageing volunteer population. The willingness of people living in the countryside to be involved in community care is not distant folk memory: it persists. But if it is to continue, it will need special kinds of help and support.' Nationally, up to 23 million adults are involved in volunteering each year. It must be said, immediately, that this figure covers voluntary help with sports and exercise, children's education, as well as the provision of health and social welfare.

The General Household Survey (GHS) 1985 produced figures to show that one adult in seven (14 per cent) was providing informal care and one in five households (10 per cent) contained a carer. This adds up to a total of 6 million carers carrying out a range of tasks: intimate domestic and personal care, supervision, juggling both personal and family relationships plus coping with pressures relating to employment, social and leisure activities. Of those 6 million, census material from 1988 identified 1.7 million carers living in the same house as the person cared for and, very surprisingly, 66 per cent receiving no help whatsoever.

Specifically rural data come from work in North Wiltshire. A significantly higher proportion (65 per cent) than in the GHS survey

(45 per cent) 'were devoting 50 hours a week or more to caring tasks, with very few (7 per cent) caring for someone in their own homes devoting less than 50 hours a week to caring tasks'.

Sir Roy Griffiths, in setting down his *Agenda for Action* in 1988, noted that the majority of care is provided by families, friends and neighbours and that 'the first task of the publicly provided services is to support and where possible strengthen those networks of carers'. But there are three potential problems for community care in rural areas.

The first results from social change in the countryside. In rural areas 68 per cent of volunteers are women. (This figure rises to 77 per cent for volunteers involving in 'caring' activities.) But it is becoming increasingly difficult to recruit volunteers. The Volunteer Centre cites several recurring problems: 'higher mortgage rates, poll tax and general cost of living mean that women have to take paid work'. So women as traditional carers in the countryside are faced with massive additional burdens or an alternative which is in fact rarely possible – relinquishing their informal caring role.

Jumble sale in Chulmleigh, Devon
(James Ravilious, Beaford Archive)

Second, there is an increasingly elderly population experiencing all the usual problems of old age, and a shortage of voluntary organisations able or willing to operate in isolated districts. Evidence from the 'more accessible' countryside points to an additional influx of newly retired people. Jean Whitaker, who has had charge of services to elderly people in south Norfolk, describes a consequence of this in-migration: 'They are fine until they reach their seventies and then they find, for one reason or another, that they can no longer drive. Often they have no relatives near and suddenly they cannot cope.' One of the problems – common to rural policy as a whole – is the welter of agencies, in this case delivering health and care services, which have a bearing on an individual: GPs, specialist physicians, district and community psychiatric nurses, health visitors, area and hospital social workers, family support services, meals-on-wheels, day-care providers, chiropodist, physio, speech and occupational therapists, voluntary agencies and clergy. There is a further difficulty for the would-be recipient in that medicine and welfare services are seen as distinct entities, to be considered and delivered separately.

Rural Voice puts its finger on the third stumbling block: too many proposals flounder 'because the theory has been worked out prior to talking to local practitioners, or local practitioners have hit a glass ceiling as their proposals for integration have run into immutable policy decisions at higher levels, in organisations or government'.

An editorial from the magazine *Community Care*, for example, bemoaned the effects of universal norms laid down by government.

> Domiciliary services, like meals on wheels or home-helps play a vital role in rural areas, perhaps doing more in terms of combating loneliness and keeping contact than might be expected of them in urban areas. Thus the suggested 12 home-helps per 1,000 of the population seems unrealistic against such a setting. Likewise day-care needs a radical rethinking

when DSS guidelines fail to allow for greater distances.

This touches on the cost of rural provision and on who should pick up the bill. It remains a moot point as to whether the traditional self-reliance of rural communities has been dictated by limited resources for outside help, or whether self-help has provided a convenient excuse for restricted assistance from external sources.

'Put at its most crude, distance is one of the main differences between rural areas and urban areas. If there is a lot of it between you and a service that you need then there is an additional cost that must be borne, either by you or by the person providing the service.' This is the summary from a 1991 Sussex RCC bulletin *Health and Care*. Rural Voice agrees that it

> often costs more to provide services in rural areas, with a lower rate of success, because populations are further apart, widely spread, and time and money is lost in travelling to/from delivery points. This is not a reason for inertia; proper planning of services requires consideration of what the rural premium is, and this needs to be built into service planning

by public or voluntary sector providers.

Partnership between Agencies Delivering Services

In 1990 a group was set up, serviced by Hampshire RCC, to look at ways of encouraging the effective delivery of health and community care in rural areas of the county. The emphasis was very much on collaboration between service providers. This co-operation grew out of earlier joint-working, leading to the publication of Hampshire's *Rural Development Strategy* in 1989 (referred to more fully in Chapter 6). Two initiatives illustrate successful partnerships between different players.

Hampshire Social Services employed an officer for one year to work in the rural parishes of Basingstoke and Deane Boroughs. The goal was to determine how social workers could be more responsive in an area where referrals were low. The work was mainly with elderly people, helping to involve them in respite and local provision. 'The project led to more productive contacts with general practitioners and health visitors and a better quality of involvement for social services which has gained an improved knowledge of local resources and networks', comments Rachel Billings of Hampshire RCC.

In Petersfield a voluntary organisation, Age Concern, installed a laundry in sheltered housing at a cost of £3,000. This was primarily for use by home care staff and carers, especially with heavy loads for elderly people in outlying areas. But the laundry is also available to young homeless people living in bed and breakfast accommodation – broadening the concept of care in the community. 'Common sense, when defined as common practice and common skills, and creative thinking are the two assets from which each of the examples outlined here benefits. These, together with the rural premium on budgets, are the prerequisites for developing the most effective means of health and community care service delivery in rural areas', concludes Rachel Billings.

> Much of our individual telephone work involves allowing carers to work through their feelings and consider their own needs. The Project's existence gives them status and recognition and, ultimately, the confidence and strength to articulate those needs and secure the necessary services to meet them.
>
> *Suffolk Carers Support Project, 1991*

The Suffolk Project (SCSP) was established in 1988 in response to comments received from carers who felt that most support was focused on the sick or disabled, and that those trying to look after them were largely left to their own devices. The scheme ran until October 1990 and was supported by the East and West Suffolk Health Authorities, Rural Development Commission and County Social Services Department. Practical support for carers, advice on their needs to statutory and voluntary bodies, and increased participation in policy-making, were all benefits of this initiative.

Self-help carers groups, established under the aegis of SCSP, represent a lifeline in reducing isolation, sharing information and giving and receiving support. One carer deliberately did not 'go on holiday until Tuesday as that would have meant missing my meeting, which I could not do. It has saved my bacon, meeting others

who understand what it is like. I am not so isolated and I am sure
that I am more cheerful. I can even help others telling them about my
experiences.'

There was a general feeling that a great deal had been achieved but
that lack of time and resources were raising expectations and forcing
workers to respond rather than initiate activities. 'The special needs
of ethnic minority carers must be given consideration. We are also
beginning to think about the needs of young carers and those carers
of people with HIV/Aids', commented the evaluation of this project
in 1991. Low expectations, entrenched gender attitudes, lack of
choice and transport have emerged as the most significant barriers for
carers, requiring further attention to overcome their effects.

One carer summed up the benefits from the Suffolk Carers
Project: 'someone has thrown me a lifeline.... The doctors, nurses
and physios – everyone is caring for my husband. Now I know if I am
feeling down I can pick up the phone and there is someone caring for
me as well.'

The 'Circle of Care' is another 'pilot' project for carers, operating
in North Wiltshire and funded to the end of 1994. It represents a
collaboration between health authorities, social services, church,
voluntary groups and local people.

Robin Osmond, who evaluated the 'Circle of Care' project
comments that this venture

> was fortunate to find someone who, through her personal drive
> and commitment...was able to address the broad and
> uncertain agenda of a new carers' organisation. This was
> particularly important as the prospective clientele was largely
> unknown to local professionals, their agencies or services, and
> invisible within the wider community and local population.

Practical information courses, a 'sitting' service for carers of people
suffering from Alzheimer's Disease and a home visiting facility were
three very practical outcomes of the work. Robin Osmond adds that
'the single most important function of the "Circle of Care" has been
to provide a focal point specifically for carers and a responsive and

reliable source of advice and information in the area'. He concludes 'that small voluntary organisations cannot go it alone and that support for carers can only be achieved through a partnership between the statutory and voluntary organisations and local community... but the reverse is happening with increasingly centralised services provided in larger towns'. The evaluation report considers that the 'Circle' should continue as a co-ordinating organisation rather than directly managing services, enabling practical information and support groups for carers, contributing to training for professionals and carers employed in the statutory services, and encouraging carer involvement and participation.

Partnership for Counselling

The Derwent Rural Counselling Service (DRCS) is an independent body that started operating in 1989. It offers professional counselling to people living in the southern part of the Derbyshire Peak District. A total of 77 clients were seen between 1989 and 1990, from 32 villages and hamlets. The majority were suffering mental distress resulting from marital or personal problems. Five professionally trained counsellors serviced the project in a voluntary capacity. Clients could, if they wished, make a donation towards the service provided.

Most of the counsellors had worked in urban areas and did not believe that a unique set of rural problems existed. In DRCS they found themselves dealing with general problems that 'rurality' perhaps skewed or amplified. There was agreement that clients of rural counselling were potentially more out-on-a-limb and confused – ' "you're not supposed to have a problem in the country"; are likely to be more isolated, geographically and socially; are likely to find support services more difficult to reach; and are more likely to be distanced from family or origin, making the "loss of something" that much more difficult to handle.'

A sample of 10 users indicated that counselling sessions had, at least, been 'useful' and, at best, 'of enormous help'. And none of these clients believed that other providers, such as social services, GP or local vicar, could have given this sort of help. 'Counselling helped me with the fear . . . it's the admission of problems to a stranger, the actual talking . . . hearing yourself say the "frightful thing" '; this is how one client described the value of the service.

And the child and family psychiatrist supervising the counsellors, agreed that the 'service appears to be filling a gap between what is offered by primary health care services and the all too rare psychotherapeutic services in the NHS. They offer an easily available . . . service which is non-threatening because it isn't labelled with the terms "psychiatry" or "psychology".'

Lateral Thinking

Carol Young, head of the NCVO Rural Team, observes that 'lateral thinking and new ways of working are needed. Some rural projects provide models of best practice which can be used by urban practitioners as well. Rural provision does not automatically imply costly delivery.'

Age Concern in Cornwall has issued CB radios to frail, elderly people
(James Ravilious, Beaford Archive)

The Herefordshire Miscarriage Helpline, for example, operates with a grant of just £500. The Helpline is staffed by volunteers who have recovered from miscarriage, and offers a vital source of support for women. By contrast, Age Concern in Cornwall has issued CB radios to frail, elderly people. A volunteer contacts each one at a set time every day, to check that all is well.

Although there are encouraging signs of sensitively organised rural community care schemes, Carol Young remains concerned about 'the lack of understanding of rural realities on the part of urban-based planners and service providers, the tendency towards high cost and lack of local services, the absence of support for rural voluntary action and the difficulties in making appropriate provision to rural communities'.

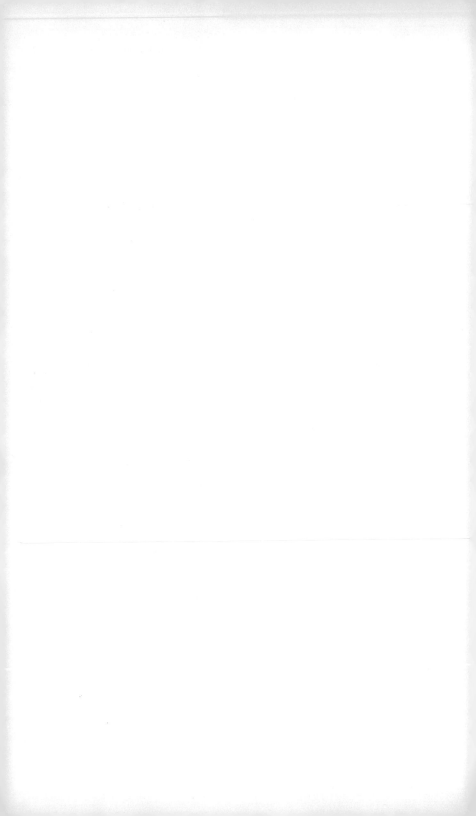

Part three

A way forward

Chapter 6

Rural Life Fights Back

One prospect that I cannot accept is the abandonment of a long-standing
tradition of a countryside that works in every sense. To settle for a passive
countryside, used only like a carpet on the floor, or a painting on the wall,
would be to fail to realise the potential of a national resource. Rural
England requires a broadly based economic and social vitality of its own.

Lord Shuttleworth, Chairman of the
Rural Development Commission, 1992

In June 1992 the British Government committed itself to integrated
policy formulation at a national, regional and local level, taking into
account environmental, social, demographic and economic issues.
This approach was finally endorsed, after much wrangling, at the
United Nations Conference on the Environment and Development
(the 'Earth Summit') held in Rio de Janeiro.

Michael Dower, the Countryside Commission's Director General,
has brought this issue from the global to the parochial:

> What do I mean by 'integrated'? I am talking about the ability
> to see things as wholes, as unities, in which the parts are
> interdependent...a village is a unity. It must offer its
> inhabitants not only homes but jobs, services, social activity,
> religion, beauty and nature, a sense of history. As it develops
> and changes, it needs to sustain a balance within this unity.

But government, as we saw in chapter 2, seems to find it virtually
impossible to see things whole, especially if that includes rural order,
and to relate to small-scale unities such as a village or parish. This is

because throughout Europe, authority is split into 'Kennomeat Chunks' – sectoral departments, and also among different tiers of national, regional and local activity. This leads directly to disunity and a *dis*-integrated approach to the application of rural policy. The present chapter demonstrates that while the symptoms of poor co-ordination are all too clear, as evidenced by rural poverty and homelessness, there are some examples of visionary activity in terms of rural development policy and practice.

The Peak District Integrated Rural Development (IRD) Project, 1981–8

The Peak Park IRD experiment was one of 12 'pilot' projects funded by the European Commission in six member states. Its objectives were to explore alternative systems of public support to deliver integrated action, thereby attempt to engage local people in defining their own proposals and then rigorously assess the results and draw conclusions for the Peak Park, rural areas of England and the Community as a whole. The project worked in three areas: the villages of Monyash (population 271) in the limestone area of the Peak, Longnor (375 people) in the Staffordshire section of the National Park and the two scattered parishes of Derwent and Hope Woodlands.

The bald facts are impressive – in relation to business development alone 60 new full-time job equivalents were generated; all housed in 10 formerly underused premises. Forty-three different community schemes were assisted, ranging from the reintroduction of local customs such as 'well dressing' in certain villages, to repairing a market cross and establishing a conservation garden. Detailed evaluation of the IRD initiative by Aston University drew particular attention to its effect on farming and land management. Generally 'there was a radical change in perceptions from one which saw the presence of wild flowers in pasture as a sign of poor farming, and therefore something to be ashamed of, to one which sees them as a positive benefit and something to be proud of'. Additionally 1,689

Dennis Mycock, using local limestone to rebuild a drystone
wall in Monyash, Derbyshire
(Peak National Park)

metres of new drystone walls were built and 152 hectares of flower
rich meadows sympathetically managed.

Beyond these very practical achievements the IRD project argues
powerfully for three 'magic ingredients' vital to rural revival. These
so-called '3 Is' are interdependence, individuality and involvement.

1 Interdependence should be based on partnerships between agencies, and on simplified grant schemes, whereby an applicant completes one form to gain access to the range of assistance on offer.

2 Recognising the individuality of different areas demands close collaboration between outside bodies and local communities. 'Forging such partnerships is clearly crucial if the individual characteristics of local areas are to be exploited to achieve their full potential', concluded the Aston research.

3 Involvement of all the relevant players is essential to the success of sustainable rural development. Commitment comes through participation; self-regeneration fosters community confidence and grants can be paid out to reward and consolidate achievement.

So the Peak Park initiative records specific achievements, based on a framework of three interlocking principles.

Hampshire Rural Development Strategy

Hampshire is not eligible for European regional assistance and does not have a Rural Development Area (RDA) within its boundaries. So with no external financial inducements Hampshire County Council in 1987 started to take a close look at rural development issues. The reason for this was concern over the 'accelerating rate of physical, economic and social change' and the lack of a 'common vision of what the future of the countryside might or should be'. Twelve working parties, tackling subjects as diverse as employment, housing, noisy sports and woodland management, drew in 140 'volunteers' from public, private and charitable sector bodies with an interest in the future of the Hampshire countryside. The result was a *Rural Development Strategy*, published in 1991. So were all the meetings and reports of any practical value? Sarah Day, the County Council's Rural Development Officer, is convinced that

the greatest benefit has been increased understanding between agencies and an appreciation of why certain bodies have particular priorities. The County recognised that it was not in control of the major players, whose activities related to many of the changes overtaking rural Hampshire. For this reason a new group, which was not part of the Council, was favoured to monitor and review progress.

Lord Selborne chairs that independent Committee for Rural Hampshire, which includes representatives from 10 countryside agencies. The Committee meets three times a year and is carrying forward the ideas of the 1991 Rural Strategy; in particular promoting 'a just and fair balance in the use and management of Hampshire's rural resources' and the maintenance of 'balanced rural communities'. Its ability to influence change is based upon the links that 'individual members forge and maintain through their various organisations'. Currently five working groups, covering adult education, enterprise, agriculture and marketing, rural housing plus health and community care, are reporting to the main Committee.

Much of the guidance and direction from the *Rural Development Strategy* has been incorporated into the new country Structure Plan. More specifically, a small Rural Enterprise Fund (£28,000 in 1992/3) has been set up to grant aid projects such as Odiham community open learning centre (near Hook, Hampshire), where computer training is offered to local people.

Sarah Day feels that 'the effort has been well worthwhile – the fact that different players on the rural scene can now relate as individuals rather than as impersonal agencies 'squaring-off' at each other, is a real step forward'. During November 1992 David Clark showed that 11 English counties (including Hampshire) had completed rural development strategies. Another three were in the pipeline. In the same month English Nature and the Rural Development and Countryside Commissions published guidelines on *Rural Strategies*:

Preparing a Rural Strategy will focus action and effort, but the document is only a beginning. It is essential that the process continues. This will enable the strategy and actions associated with it to maintain momentum and ensure a continuing partnership approach to achieve a more secure future for the rural environment and the rural communities that live within it.

From the public to the charitable sector, evidence of strategic thinking about rural issues is evident.

Rural Action: Voluntary Not Amateur

There are 38 Rural Community Councils (RCCs) – one in each English shire county. RCCs promote the welfare of rural people by encouraging self-help, local initiatives and voluntary effort. Working alongside other bodies they offer practical advice to village hall committees, parish or town councils, plus other groups and individuals. In 1989 community councils were in touch with 11,000 parishes, 9,000 halls and many schools, youth groups, Women's Institutes and local voluntary organisations. This constitutes a wide network as a basis for action with communities in rural England.

Professor W.G.S. Adams in 1922 wrote perhaps the abiding definition of RCC work:

> The tendency has been on the one hand to give the village what was considered good for it and, on the other, to turn to someone else for help on all occasions. The essence of the country problem is to find means to enable country men and women to help themselves, and to bring together all classes in co-operation for the common good.

During 1991 Peter Newell, Director of the RCC in Wiltshire, offered a variation on this theme:

> We receive financial support from local authorities, government departments, charitable trusts and commerce, but remain an independent organisation managed by local people, staffed by a team of experts. The RCC tries to explore new ways of helping people to live and work in their own villages and small

towns. We set up projects ourselves and help other groups to find resources, including finance, for their own work.

A race through the activities of this RCC gives a flavour of the initiatives in progress. During 1991 the community council had five constituent development projects under its wing plus another five subsidiary companies. At one level the community council administers around £100,000 of county council money for major and minor repair work to village halls; then there are two area-based community development projects serving East and West Kennet respectively. Janet Horner in East Kennet worked with local people to revive the flagging Jubilee Centre at Marlborough, by guiding them through the maze of legal and insurance requirements plus charitable registration. Chair of the centre, Lois De Lyle-Turner, is convinced that 'without Janet's continuous guidance, patience and dedication to her work, the task of reviving the centre would have been extremely difficult'.

During 1990–1 the RCC's Rural Initiatives Fund paid out £5,735 towards 29 small community projects. On the housing front, since 1988, the community council-inspired Wiltshire Rural Housing Association has completed 54 homes to accommodate 130 people in Tilshead, Codford, Winterslow, Minety, Mildenhall, Leigh, Kingston Langley, Hindon, Rushall and Luckington. More are going up at Edington, Castle Combe and Milton Lilbourne. Mr and Mrs Davis are happy to be living in one of the Minety properties: 'Before, we were living a three-bedroomed council house with my mother and father, my brother, nephew and our two daughters. The baby had her cot in our room but we had to have her sister in our bed. It's lovely to have more space.'

The community council's employment and enterprise initiatives target those who are disadvantaged in looking for work; they aim to foster community-based action and flexible service delivery.

Young entrepreneurs from 250 businesses, employing over 290 staff, have been given detailed practical assistance in setting-up since the Youth Enterprise Service was launched in 1983. In addition, New Opportunities for Women has provided training and practical experience in marketing and management for women returners. Using European Social Fund money, contributions from local government and the private sector, this project is pioneering skills training and job placements tailored to the needs of women living in rural Wiltshire. In addition a new Rural Women's Project is being targeted on groups of smaller villages, operating with local people to assess the needs and opportunities of women, bring a variety of appropriate, informal, training into the village and pursue job search and self-employment approaches to making a living.

Workout has assisted more than 3,500 redundant, early-retired and unemployed people into gainful employment. A joint venture with local authorities, it aims to help employees experiencing significant changes in their work pattern, for example through short-time employment, lengthy sick leave or family problems. Redundancy counselling and advice on alternative job opportunities have been provided for employees from such industrial giants as Bowyers in Trowbridge, Wilton Royal Carpets, Rover, GEC and Royal Mail. A five-year contract has now been secured from the Ministry of Defence to assist civilians made redundant through military cuts.

Third Age First was established in 1989 by the RCC to provide specialist employment advice and support for the over-fifties. More than 1,000 have registered for work, of whom some 500 have been successfully placed into employment. Third Age First has created New Directions Training which covers such issues as financial management, health, skills assessment, friendship networks and personal responsibility. This combines group work and individual counselling.

Although Melksham Workspace existed for just two years, it enabled 17 new businesses to set up in a supportive environment with on-site business advice and support services. The majority of tenants were over 50 years of age, younger people or those previously made redundant. Unfortunately, as anticipated, the owners ultimately needed the property for their own requirements and the premises shut down early in 1991. However, Richard Earle of Oriel Systems was able to record a successful move from Workspace to new offices in

Corsham. 'We may be small but we are now exporting computer software. Without Workspace we would never have made the break.'

The community council has also sponsored the production of a series of 21 video films on rural subjects through the television and video production unit, Trilith, which it established. Trilith is undertaking research into the potential of cable TV as a community resource in the countryside.

Mere Telecottage, a community computing and communications facility, was opened in a village library by the RCC. Wiltshire County Council, British Telecom and Barclays Bank have all given financial assistance. Launched in 1991, the 'telecottage' offers a full range of modern office and communications equipment for use by small businesses plus community groups, and provides training in computer skills for local people. A second telecottage is now operating in Codford with a third at an advanced stage of preparation at Crudwell.

New Heart for Ilfracombe

The report of my death was an exaggeration

Mark Twain

Ilfracombe is a Victorian seaside resort of 11,000 people on the rugged North Devon coast. Project Officer Helen Dimond describes it as 'an inner-city ghetto marooned in a sea of prosperous countryside, with high unemployment and associated social problems'. The heyday of Ilfracombe town was between 1880 and 1914 when train and steamer-loads of visitors flocked from Wales and Bristol. Helen Dimond sees the seeds of accelerating decline in the shift towards dependence on tourism: 'Staying visitors have decreased in number, giving way to day-trippers, and the town has to compete for these with other attractions. In bleak moments you feel as though you're just rearranging deckchairs on the Titanic.' Towards the end of the 1980s 'about one in three of the local population was registered unemployed. The number of young people out of work was up around 50 per cent.'

But since this low point the town has begun to get back on its feet. The start of the Ilfracombe Project was greeted with mixed omens. In May 1986 several hundred people crowded into the Pavilion Theatre on Cup Final Day to help it on its way; but on the very first night of Civic Trust involvement in the town the Beacon Castle Hotel went up in flames! Since then the revival of Ilfracombe has been a much steadier undertaking. For the first three years the Trust – a campaigning environmental charity – led the Project at the invitation of North Devon District Council. The District has now taken up the reins, with the Civic Trust providing support.

The aim of the initiative is to reverse the trend of physical and economic decline which has affected the town since 1914. It has done this through improvements to buildings, open spaces, arts ventures, new development, landscaping, traffic management, economic and community ventures. Helen Dimond acknowledges that 'there is much to do, and limited money to spend. The Project Team is tiny and could hardly act alone. Its role is that of a catalyst. It succeeds through persuasion, relying on partnership and the support of local people. The revival of Ilfracombe draws strength from the appeal of the town's built heritage, the beautiful surrounding country and sea views.'

And the results are dramatic: between 1986 and 1989 £5 million invested in new land and buildings, £665,000 secured from charitable and other grant sources, outside funding for improvements to privately owned property set at £250,000 and additional community facilities developed at a cost of £750,000.

Large swathes of streetscape and open space have been widened, repaved, cleared of clutter and generally enhanced. The derelict URC chapel has been transformed into a community centre, aptly named 'The Lantern', housing meeting rooms, playgroup facilities and a 200-seat performance space. Seven sponsors ranging across the public, private and charitable sectors met the £600,000 bill for restoration.

Meanwhile, an old coastal radio station has become the 'Ariel' training centre for music and the performing arts. British Telecom

*The derelict URC chapel has been transformed into the Lantern
community centre in Ilfracombe, Devon
(TEK Photography)*

made over the building and financed renovation. It now houses
recording studios, practice rooms, a music project and provides
facilities for the town's marching bands. North Devon District, with
grant aid from the Rural Development Commission, has also
converted part of an old gas works into 'starter' workshops for small
businesses.

Just as important, there is a new spirit of self reliance. Local
companies have clubbed together to form a Tourism Association;
Ilfracombe Civic Society has grown from nothing to an active
membership of over 200. In 1989, as a result of extensive tree
planting and other self-help ventures, Ilfracombe came joint first
(with Sidmouth) in the Britain in Bloom competition.

A fair in the Great Hall at the Lantern community centre
(TEK Photography)

The Channel Arts Association has promoted Ilfracombe as a Festival Town. Founder Chair, Jon Bell, comments that 'establishing the National Youth Arts Festival is a deliberate attempt to involve local young people in promoting the resort. At the same time it engages the interest of a national audience who would not otherwise regard Ilfracombe as an interesting place to visit and this helps give the town a different profile'.

Helen Dimond rounds off by observing that 'The town looks

Voice and Rhythm Workshop run by the Half Moon Young People's Theatre for participants at the National Youth Arts Festival (Channel Arts Association)

better, and local confidence is returning. The activity of the past few years has started to turn the tide for Ilfracombe, but the longer-term future depends on much more being accomplished.'

Allenheads: Resurrection of a Dying Village

'When we came there was a host of estate workers, there wasn't a wall down or a stone out of place; now there are no workers at all. When the mines were going it used to be a 'clang and clatter' in that yard the whole time. Now it's all silent. Allenheads is a village of

*Northcote Buildings, Church Street, a terrace of houses and shops
built in 1880 and typical of Ilfracombe's Victorian Heritage
(Civic Trust)*

pensioners – a dying village.' This was the view of one elderly resident
of England's highest village in 1985. It could have been the epitaph
for any number of upland communities in Britain. It was a call to
arms for Allenheads (population 160), which lies at the meeting
point of Cumbria, Durham and Northumberland.

In October 1985 the *Newcastle Journal* prompted locals into
action: 'Tragic and hopeless are the words you hear when the experts
are talking about Allenheads. The village they say is sinking slowly
but surely into oblivion.'

Bob Maddison, a local watercolour artist, convened a village
meeting which pulled in a good third of the population. The
Allenheads Action Committee was the unlikely but effective result,

comprising an OAP, one unemployed person, publican, gamekeeper and housewife. Local opinion on the needs and aspirations of the community was canvassed using a household questionnaire. Results 'showed that 92 per cent of people were in favour of trying to attract more tourists to Allenheads and felt this would benefit the local economy'.

Many places would then have sat back and let 'the authorities' pick up the reins. But Allenheads has a peculiar alchemy: David Flush, a resident and ex-employee of British Steel, found himself propelled into the driving seat – he worked as a volunteer, getting the Allenheads project off the ground. David Flush continued the venture through the government's Community Programme and, eventually, the Allenheads Trust became his employer. The Trust draws strength from the village that it serves: 107 adults and 26 children (83 per cent of the total population are members). Designation of the North Pennines as England's largest Area of Outstanding Natural Beauty (AONB) also opened up new possibilities for outside financial support.

Lord Allendale owns 99 per cent of the village, not to mention 30,000 acres of surrounding grouse moor; the estate's contribution has been crucial to the turn-around in Allenheads. One prominent building was given to the community – the estate stayed its hand over demolishing the property and selling the stone to a nearby mining museum. David Flush says: 'As the Allendale estate has realised how serious we are about our own future and as they have seen the practical results of our hard work, so they have become increasingly helpful.'

With advice from the Northumberland Rural Development Programme, the community set about feasibility studies of two redundant buildings in the village centre. David Flush recalls the meeting at which their proposals were unveiled: 'All the agencies were there and it was like a Billy Graham crusade with speaker after speaker pledging support.'

The Rural Development and Countryside Commissions, county, district and parish councils, the Allendale Estate, the then

Manpower Services Commission plus a scattering of local and regional businesses have put around £500,000 into the village between 1985 and 1991. The Old Inn now houses a community and conference centre, plus post office/shop and property for rent. The latter is intended to generate income to finance further work. The Old Stables have gone from cow byre to craft workshops and a cafe now operates on a franchise from the Allenheads Trust.

Beyond a children's play area is a circular nature trail, completed with help from the British Trust for Conservation Volunteers and utilising interpretation panels designed by a resident, who is also an environmental consultant. People have helped according to their talents. A pensioner, Lizzie Ridley, carried out an informal housing survey by talking with other retired residents. The upshot was a six-house development for local elderly people, built by North Housing Association. These constitute the first new houses in Allenheads for over a century! As larger homes are vacated by older occupants, families who are likely to contribute to the local economy are encouraged to move in.

A local businessman put £40,000 into the restoration and display of a unique Armstrong Hydraulic engine. This water-powered machine, used in the lead mines during the nineteenth century, has been reconnected to its original supply and operates as a working exhibit. An old smithy has become a museum featuring the lead mining origins of the village. On the old mineyard, derelict buildings have been converted by the Allendale Estate to six workshops; these are fully occupied and house a riding tack manufacturer, frozen food business and giftware producer. New enterprises mean new jobs and greater activity in the village.

But the Allenheads Project has not been universally welcomed. As Trust Chair, Pat McMullen, commented in 1991: 'Soap opera plots have nothing on the rumours which fly around here . . . the cause of rumour is lack of facts.' At Allenheads a community appraisal triggered efforts at revival, only to be followed by a second self-analysis completed in 1992. These were undertaken with considerable backing from the Northumberland RCC. The second appraisal report recorded some opinions which demonstrated

a high level of ill will and destructiveness which is difficult to deal with in a small community. Now that it is in existence, it is open to question whether the end of the Allenheads Trust would actually solve any problems and one person's claim that 'if the clock could be turned back six years everyone would be happy' was proved false by the majority of views expressed by others.

Allenheads demonstrates that revival need not be exclusive to wealthier, larger, communities and that countryside agencies and local people can collaborate to produce astonishing results. But it is also a cautionary tale that demonstrates how rural development is not neutral; it is likely to promote some and relegate others. It is crucial to have a clear idea at the outset, as to what is intended; who will gain and who may well lose out. The alternative – to do nothing – is really no option at all: standing still is in effect falling behind as other, more dynamic communities seize the opportunities open to them.

Rural Deprivation and the Response from Voluntary Organisations

In 1992 NCVO commissioned consultants Community Contact and the Community Council of Devon 'to discover the views of voluntary organisations on the extent of disadvantage facing residents of rural areas; and to get some impression of what community agencies and groups are doing, or might like to do, to reduce them'. The research related to the activities of local, regional and national voluntary organisations as they affected six villages from Derbyshire/Staffordshire and Devon.

The 1992 research commissioned by NCVO into 'rural deprivation and voluntary organisations and groups' demonstrates how these bodies are at work in the English countryside: for example, offering counselling, ministering to the sick and lonely, helping to boost women's self-reliance, researching deprivation and helping disabled people to articulate their own needs.

In the Derbyshire/Staffordshire survey area, 30 organisations (63 per cent of respondents) worked in partnership with others to tackle aspects of disadvantage: Glossop Women's Aid collaborates with the local police, while the Peak Park Trust has engaged with Asian and Afro-Caribbean organisations to encourage access by these communities to the countryside.

Also, a significant number of the surveyed organisations (28, or 58 per cent) say they would like to do more to tackle deprivation: for example, by breaking down ignorance regarding mental illness, providing after school activities for children, taking on more 'field' workers. But as the report bluntly puts it, 'Reasons for not doing more centre on money, time and need of more volunteers.' Of 40 voluntary organisations operating within the Peak, 18 (45 per cent) rely on the vagaries of subscriptions, fundraising, sponsorship or donations.

In Devon and Derbyshire/Staffordshire 41 respondents would welcome more information about rural disadvantage, literature about training opportunities around themes of deprivation, or both. The researchers believe that 'rural voluntary organisations and groups are uniquely placed in devising strategies to tackle rural problems, not least in relation to the spatial segregation of the rurally deprived'. There is a need to explore further exactly how these information and training needs can be translated from general interest to specific action:

> The heavy reliance on volunteers which the study confirms makes for a distinct training agenda of itself. And what do management committees know, or want to know, about rural deprivation? Should there be more overt partnership arrangements between the larger, funded, and the more parochial, non-funded voluntary organisations? Can some organisations, for example the National Farmers' Union, act as a bridgehead to the effective delivery of relevant services, for example Samaritans, Relate, Low Pay Unit?

The researchers point out that policy and practice inevitably reflect, often in complex ways, different assumptions and perspectives. 'Hence, we say – beware the definition or explanation of deprivation, and voluntary action, which is taken for granted.' The NCVO study discusses the phenomenon of individuals and groups within a village being 'in different boats' which are opposed because of social structures and divisions. An understanding of these 'structural inequalities' can shed light on different patterns of voluntary action: the truism that incomers generally seek acceptance by the community through active participation, for example, seems well-founded.

> If it follows that, by dint of time, wealth, mobility, etc., some people and groups are more able to participate in voluntary action, our support for training opportunities for voluntary organisations and groups has to be located within that reality.

Derbyshire / Staffordshire

The groups canvassed ranged across a broad spectrum of interests: Women's Aid, lesbian and gay issues, Samaritans, community transport, CABx, Guides and Brownies. Of those responding to a postal questionnaire 19 per cent were run by/for women. In terms of people served there was a wide divergence between the 2,500 people using Bakewell and Eyam's community transport each month and the six attenders at Bamford Young People's Group. Twenty-nine organisations (61 per cent) employed no staff while 41 (85 per cent) depend on volunteers. Neil Shenton, of Community Contact, observes that 'the vast majority administer a budget, but of these almost half rely solely on a combination of subscriptions, fundraising, sponsorship or donations'. Of those replying 79 per cent belong to a larger organisation, Federation or Network.

Neil goes on to point out that, as far as rural deprivation is concerned, '44 respondents (92 per cent) said that it exists in the geographical areas they cover. The overwhelming definitions of "disadvantage" centre on transport problems, housing, declining services, isolation, loneliness, unemployment and low pay.' Discrimination against certain sections of society, such as homosexuals, is consistently seen as affecting very few people.

Countering Deprivation

Thirty-six organisations (75 per cent) say that they are tackling deprivation by 'asserting the needs of women'; gaining 'access to decision-makers' and 'mobilising the disabled'. Of these organisations, 58 per cent would like to do more given extra money, time and additional volunteers. Those most in need of help were identified as the elderly, young marrieds, teenagers and disabled people. At the other end of the scale 'incomers' were judged least likely to require assistance. One voluntary agency, working with young people, took this a step further by observing that 'everything is geared towards visitors, and the influx of them makes young people feel like "strangers in their own land". There is a class context to this – 'townies' turn up in flash cars and with all the latest gear that local people can't afford. There's a feeling of wanting some territory of our own.'

Devon Case Study

The Devon response was relatively small and different in character and contained far more 'social' groups (like WIs) or those centred on fundraising (such as Cancer Research) than the Peak – which included a preponderance of welfare orientated groups. Not all rural areas are the same.

Of the voluntary bodies responding 23 (82 per cent) co-ordinated the work of others or provided services direct. As with the Peak there was a wide range in terms of people served each month – the Samaritans citing 1,100 and the Mothers' Union just 16 recipients. The Devlon material mirrors that from the Peak with 64 per cent of voluntary agencies employing no staff and 82 per cent utilising volunteers.

Roughly half of the groups replying operate a budget – 73 per cent of these depending on sponsorship, donations and fundraising. Most belong to a larger Federation or Network. Gayle Kirrage, of the Community Council, comments that

> a majority of the organisations thought that deprivation exists in their area. The overwhelming indicator of 'disadvantage' was considered to be lack of transport or affordable transport. Isolation and loneliness were also rated highly, with limited amenities and housing following. Agencies believed very similar problems confronted all parts of the community. The question on incomers was largely ignored, although the responses given were highly emotive and personal.

As in the Peak elderly and disabled people, young marrieds and teenagers were felt to constitute the 'most needy'.

National Voluntary Organisations – Their Response to Rural Deprivation

Neil Shenton feels that 'an emergent theme in the returned forms from national bodies, which perhaps explains the "blanks" and "don't knows", is the stated or implied assertion that they are predominantly "urban" '. Alcohol Concern, for example, is developing an interest in rural areas, because the alcohol field has traditionally concentrated on the urban population's counselling needs.

From this localised review of rural deprivation and the response of voluntary organisations it is clear that a majority of agencies do register deprivation as a reality. On the other hand 'discrimination' against certain groups barely registered as an issue and the common plea was for greater resources to provide more effective services. In Devon, a more deeply rural area, the understanding of 'minority issues' was not as strongly articulated as in the Peak District. Generally, larger local or regional agencies displayed a greater awareness of the needs of minorities, but there was still uncertainty as to how to respond. Specialised training was seen as an essential prerequisite to appropriate action. The researchers felt that established voluntary groups, with a secure funding base, offered the best hope of raising and dealing with rural 'minority issues'.

Chapter 7

Another Country – Paradise Regained?

Before considering possible prescriptions for rural society in England let us briefly review the points made in the previous chapters.

A Green and Pleasant Land?

- The countryside is important as a national resource. Ten million people, one-fifth of England's population, live and work in rural areas.
- There is a tendency to think of villages as attractive, agricultural communities. But many are highly industrial, not necessarily well-to-do or pretty places.
- The inner cities and rural areas share problems, including low wages, pockets of high unemployment and a concentration of disadvantaged groups.
- The present influx of migrants to the countryside requires mutual respect and sensitivity on behalf of incomers and longer-standing residents alike.

Policy and Practice – The Impact of Myths

- The fact that 'rural' communities are largely seen as 'agricultural' is reflected in the virtual monopoly of public sector support for the countryside, which is channelled through to farmers.
- Although many view the country as having few problems, research points to 2 million 'disadvantaged' people – one-fifth of those in rural England – suffering low wages, poor personal mobility, access to housing and a range of services.

- Rapid repopulation of the countryside is leading to a dislocation of village life: voluntary activities cannot automatically be counted on to fill gaps left by the statutory authorities; and women as the traditional 'carers' are now choosing, or having to take on, paid work.
- Rural facilities continue to wither away: 73 per cent of English parishes have no daily bus service. As younger people leave, so older, wealthier people – who may have no need of the local school, shop or bus – are arriving in rural areas.
- Relatively high costs of providing small-scale provision to scattered communities are not always taken into account by those planning rural services.

Rural Deprivation – Fact Not Fiction

- Urban 'indicators' fail to give an accurate picture of rural concerns. Running a car is generally seen as a sign of affluence but for many rural residents it is a necessity. High petrol and maintenance costs can therefore contribute to rural disadvantage.
- Rural 'deprivation' manifests itself in a lack of low-cost housing, limited job opportunities and the presence of few specialists to help vulnerable groups such as pre-school children, disabled and elderly people.
- In the countryside 60 per cent of women do not drive. Non-existence childcare provision is another major factor which forces rural women to take on part-time or seasonal, poorly paid and insecure jobs. For many women the combination of paid work, caring and domestic duties is a formidable burden and 'juggling act'.
- Disabled people face particular problems in the countryside: most buildings are physically inaccessible to them and there is a lack of specialist staff – including physio and speech therapists. Customised provision is problematic given the differing needs of small numbers of disabled people, spread over sometimes considerable distances.

- One-tenth of the entire population is likely to experience some form of mental 'illness' during their lifetime. Of 160 occupational categories, farmers are the second most likely to commit suicide. Rural areas can suffer from a lack of trained personnel, and great distances to treatment or hospital can be a substantial barrier to rehabilitation. Attempts to counter centralised provision and to adopt non-stigmatising 'labels' for services are seen as crucial in a rural setting.
- For young people the countryside can be a 'trap'. Many experience 'claustrophobia', intolerance of unorthodox behaviour, and feel impotent to influence decisions made within the village. Dependence on parents for transport can be a further cause of friction.
- Little detailed information exists on the experience of black and ethnic minorities of the countryside. Conservatively, around 137,000 live in rural England and Wales. Understanding gained through personal experience seems crucial to breaking down any initial hostility.
- Stereotypes persist about the prevalence of (child) sex abuse in the countryside. It is important to distinguish crime committed in the countryside from that perpetrated by rural residents. The social 'closeness' of some communities can hamper attempts, by victims and offenders, to 'start afresh'.

Housing and Homelessness
- When compared with urban areas a greater proportion of houses in the countryside are in poor condition.
- Poverty leads to poor housing and diet which, in turn, contributes to mental and other ailments, particularly among the elderly.
- Six to nine 'affordable' homes are needed immediately in each of England's 8,000 villages to meet the demand for low-cost properties.
- Of registered homeless people 14 per cent live in rural areas. A report published by the Rural Development Commission in

1992 showed that between 1987 and 1991 the 'incidence of homelessness tripled in deep rural areas, and overall rural homelessness increased at a faster rate than urban homelessness'.

- The national housing crisis must be solved at a local level.

Health and Community Care

- It is a myth to suggest that no ill-health exists in the countryside.
- Partnerships between statutory and voluntary organisations and the local community are essential to deliver customised and effective services.
- Rural provision does not necessarily have to be expensive.
- Communication between health and care practitioners is essential to ensure a straightforward and organised system of service delivery.

Rural Life Fights Back

- Rural areas must be seen as 'unities' – requiring action to support their social, economic, cultural and environmental well-being.
- Collaboration is a pragmatic and appropriate requirement in addressing the needs of rural communities.
- Evidence suggests that voluntary organisations acting in the countryside must distinguish between the needs of different sections of rural society and respond accordingly.

Looking Ahead

I agree that the future of our countryside and people who live in it are of deep concern . . .

John Major responding to the Duke of Westminster's Report,
'Problems in Rural Areas', 1993

In 1988 Professor Ken Young contended that 'the widely held vision of the rural future is one which places heavy emphasis upon the visual, rather than the economic, environment. So in this sense the countryside matters – up to a point'. But he went on to argue that however strongly people might feel about the countryside 'their views remain politically irrelevant if they cannot distinguish between the positions of the several political parties . . . most tend to favour what they imagine to be the countryside policy of the party they support for other reasons. So we cannot say yet that the countryside matters in an electoral sense.'

David Clark has studied the election returns from 66 predominantly rural seats between 1974 and 1992. The Conservatives share of the rural vote has never dropped below 53.5 per cent since they formed a government in 1979. This is reflected in the Tories' super-dominance of seats, taking 66 out of 69 in 1979 and 62 from a total of 66 in 1992. By contrast, the Labour Party has trailed in third, in terms of rural votes, at every election since 1974. Even when Labour won in 1974 it polled just 25.3 per cent of the rural vote. In 1992 they secured only 17.1 per cent (up from the 1983 all-time-low of 11.6 per cent). In the 1992 General Election Labour was 10 per cent behind the Liberal Democrats, and a whopping 36 per cent short of the Conservatives. There appears to be Tory invincibility in the shires, while Labour has ceased to be a credible contender for rural seats.

In July 1992 Audrey Lees, recent Chair of ACRE, called for a rural charter to 'raise and guarantee the quality of rural living and give the assurance that village life will endure and prosper'. She stressed the need for achievable targets to be set and cited several rhetorical examples such as

> at least one doctor's surgery open six days a week within three miles? Provision of housing for rent at a given proportion of average earnings? At least a twice-daily public transport link to a small town with good services? Surely goals like these will promote the thinking that is needed to deliver rural services effectively and economically.

A Tory MP, David Porter, has sought a complementary 'rural audit of all policies' which would produce from government 'a considered rural policy, wide in scope and as integrated as possible, which automatically considers the effects on the countryside of proposed legislation and spending programmes'.

The March of European Influence

While at a national level rural issues have taken a 'back seat', within Europe there has been much more urgency in dealing with these concerns. The presence of Ireland, Portugal and Greece among 'the 12' has significantly tilted the centre of gravity back towards the country areas. As the European Council for the Village and Small Town (ECOVAST), a pan-European body promoting the well-being of villages and protecting the rural heritage, points out in its 1991 *Strategy for Rural Europe*: 'The countryside of Europe covers 85 per cent of the continent's land area, and contains the homes of more than half of its people.' Ray MacSharry, recent EC Commissioner for Agriculture and Rural Development, went on to say that 'We cannot tolerate the impoverishment of rural areas outside the mainstream.... Their economic and social needs have been neglected far too long. They must be given the opportunity to both contribute to and benefit from economic development just as fully as the urban population.'

However, when areas were first designated in 1989 under Objective 5b – specifically encouraging rural development – only the Scottish Highlands and Islands, part of Dumfries and Galloway, Mid Wales plus a tiny portion of Devon and Cornwall were eligible for this European assistance. The vast majority of rural England, therefore, including the 29 Rural Development and Coalfield Closure Areas supported by national government, were not able to tap into this additional EC countryside aid package, although some have benefited under other programmes, such as supporting declining industrial areas and projects for women.

During 1990 Brussels compounded this concentration on 5b and other areas lagging behind (including the whole of Ireland and Greece) by selecting around 100 local agencies to receive help under a new LEADER (*Liaison entre actions de développement de l'économie rurale*) programme. Guidelines on LEADER stressed 'the need to take into account all aspects of rural society, the way they interact as well as the variety of local situations within the community [the principle of the *Integrated approach* in contrast to the sectoral approach]'. But in practice this strategy for rural development would be 'largely geared to the role of agriculture and forestry in the countryside'.

What this points to is a laudable intention to assist rural development but one which loses something in the translation between different European partners. It also demonstrates the continuing confusion or interchangeability between 'agricultural' and 'rural' development. Direct European support for the latter remains irrelevant to all but a tiny portion of rural England. The English countryside is seen as being too 'urban' because its agricultural workforce is so small. The case for EC rural assistance therefore remains problematic.

Nevertheless, at an informal level, there is much to learn from our European neighbours in terms of devolving power to the localities and in developing specific initiatives aimed at reviving the rural economy.

Local government: home and away

> England: Parish Councils are important building blocks in any
> future local government structure.
> *Sir John Banham, 1992*

On the homefront, parish or town councils, the level of government closest to the people, are commonly perceived as something of a joke. The Local Government Review, headed by Sir John Banham, has been seen as a battleground between the county and district councils, with the parishes gaining little practical recognition. A 1992 Green Paper concluded that the range and diversity of these local councils militated against across-the-board increases in their rights and powers. The door was left ajar for some of the larger councils to apply to take on all or some of the functions of district or county councils for their area. Bedfordshire County Council has struck a deal with Dunstable Town Council (population 35,000) in which responsibility for the arts, museums, youth service and some grant aid in Dunstable will pass to the local council.

Contrary to their 'Mickey Mouse' tag, the third tier of local government can exercise considerable power. A 1992 survey, *Parish and Town Councils in England*, showed that while some councils are run entirely on a voluntary basis with no paid staff and little expenditure, others represent communities of over 30,000 people, may have a budget of more than £1 million and expenditure and staffing levels per head of population similar to the smaller district councils.

There are 8,159 local councils in England with 70,000 elected representatives – more than three times the number of district and county councillors. Around half of the parishes provide churchyards, notice boards, seats, outdoor recreational facilities, village greens and community halls. The services directly supported by local councils in 1989/90 are shown in Figure 5 and although larger

Figure 5 Services on which parish and town councils spent money in 1989/90

Percentage of councils spending money on:

• Churchyards/burial facilities	• Lighting	• Comunity surveys
• Signs and notice-boards	• Dealing with litter	• Allotments
• Seats and shelters	• War memorials	• Roadside verges
• Outdoor recreation	• Information services	
• Open spaces/ greens/commons	• Local newsletters	
• Village/community halls	• Entering competitions	
	• Maintaining footpaths	
47–56%	28–33%	19–23%

Source: S. Ellwood et al., *Parish and Town Councils in England: A Survey*, HMSO, 1992

councils tend to provide a more extensive range, provision by the smallest authorities is also extensive.

Of all the parish and town councils 75 per cent own land or buildings including 33 per cent of the smallest ones. In 1990 local councils in England held an estimated £100 million. On the negative side though, while councils were more active in the 1987–90 elections than in 1964, still only 44 per cent of seats were contested. And turnover of councillors is high – 43 per cent of parishes reported vacancies in 1989/90.

So the picture emerges of latent as well as actual potential among the parish and town councils of England. And as Alexis de Tocqueville concluded in 1835 in his study of democracy:

> The strength of free peoples resides in the local community. Local institutions are to liberty what primary schools are to science; they put it within the people's reach; they teach people to appreciate its peaceful enjoyment and accustom them to make use of it. Without local institutions a nation may give itself a free government but it has not got the spirit of liberty.

Professor John Stewart from Birmingham University highlights the fact that local authorities in Europe

> are first and foremost representative of communities. The word 'commune' expresses a concept of local government as the community governing itself. As such the local authority has the power of general competence...to take any action on behalf of the community that is not specifically barred. It is the reverse of the position in this country where local authorities normally need specific powers.

Denmark

Ejgil Rasmussen is the elected mayor and head of administration for the municipality of Gedved in Jutland. Danish local government underwent substantial reorganisation in 1970 when 1,300 municipalities were merged into a total of just 275. Gedved, for example, is composed of four former authorities; it takes in 9,600 people and covers 14,000 hectares – roughly one-sixth of that covered by a district council such as South Norfolk. In Denmark 128 municipalities have a population of only 5,000–10,000. But unlike their English equivalent – the town councils – Gedved is responsible for the care of 1,700 pensioners and for old people's homes. Additionally, municipalities run primary schools, leisure time activities, libraries, cultural and sporting facilities. They also maintain local roads and arrange gas, electricity and water supplies. The fire service, rubbish collection and sewerage control are other municipal functions exercised locally. Tim Cawkwell, who organised a 'Parish Government in Rural Europe' conference during 1991, notes that 'a picture emerges of considerably greater responsibility being exercised at the local level than in this country... the crucial element in the system is the fact that the municipality has an important power to collect taxes for itself as well as for the state and county'.

France

By contrast there are 36,000 Maires (Mayors) in France. Of these 32,000 preside over 'communes' of fewer than 2,000 people. They are supported by 150,000 adjoints (deputies) and 500,000 councillors. For example, the commune of Ambierle near St-Etienne maintains nearly 150 kilometres of roads and public buildings including churches, schools and village halls. Furthermore it is responsible for the supply of water and assists with local education.

Ambierle employs six staff carrying out building maintenance and four teachers. The mayor is responsible for overall planning of the area and s/he also grants necessary planning permissions. Tim Cawkwell observes that 'since 1991 France has been consciously trying to decentralise power and give more authority to mayors... four local taxes contribute around 50 per cent of a Commune's budget: domestic rates, a levy on built property and undeveloped land plus a tax on businesses'. The other half of a local budget is made up by the state. In UK terms the financial clout of these small communities is mouth-watering: Ambierle, for example, in 1991 operated a budget of £505,000. But even enthusiasts for local action might feel that 32,000 authorities of under 2,000 population was taking devolution too far.

From Policy to Practice

Sweden

Bengt Dahlgren, an economic development officer from western Sweden, points out that 'it is easy to see how marginal area policy stimulates entrepreneurship, how the power of initiative grows, how the desire to experiment flourishes and the imagination is stirred. New thoughts are thought and new things are done.' The Swedes have a great deal of new ideas. For example, in the pretty lake-side community of Gräsmark in Värmland County the church has always been a favourite with couples. The locals decided to exploit this by marketing their own 'wedding package', including traditional service, costumes, live music, use of wooden reception cabin and honeymoon accommodation. Such a simple idea has generated about 10 weddings every year. If at each wedding there are an average of 50 guests there are then 500 extra visitors, utilising local hotels and services, than would otherwise be the case. And as Inger Axelsson, the local councillor behind the project, comments, 'the beauty is that the village determines how many staying guests it can cope with and spreads these accordingly'.

Meanwhile, some way from the central Swedish city of Östersund lies the tiny village of Lövvik (population: 50). Resident Helmer Jansson takes up the story:

> In 1940 the population of Lövvik was roughly 250 people. By 1960 the number had dropped to 125. Today it is close to 50 – an increase since 1988 when there were just 35 inhabitants. Like many other villages all the public facilities have been stripped, including the school, post office, country store, taxi and bus service.

The age structure of the population is not ideal either – 10 people under 20, 20 between 45 and 65 and another 20 in retirement. The response from Lövvik has been quite extraordinary. In 1990 the village started its own co-operative, leading to the opening in October 1991 of a community-run home for eight elderly people.

The 'home' cost 4.7 million Swedish kroner (£470,000) to complete and was paid for with bank loans. The co-operative of 16 members has carried out an enormous amount of the physical work itself (2,500 hours on such things as building and decorating). The co-op employs six women, who are all modestly paid an identical wage, to staff the home – cooking, caring and running the administration.

The Kommun (local authority) contributes monthly rents of 30,400 Swedish kroner (£3,040) for the residents. This is considerably cheaper for the Kommun than moving local people to a central facility in the nearest town of Strömsund with, for example, its much greater staff overheads.

Lövvik boasts the first 'elder co-operative' in Sweden and it is now being copied by other communities. The elderly residents sit on a 'steering committee', alongside another 16 co-op members, and can thereby influence decisions made about the running of 'their' centre.

Although the Lansstyrelsen (County Council) has paid for some of the furniture and the Kommun underwrites the project, it has succeeded mainly because of local determination. There is also an open acknowledgement of self-interest, by a number of the middle-aged volunteers, that 'in a few years' time this will be our home'. Eight houses have been 'released', allowing relatives of the residents to live close by and to help at the home. This has the double benefit of increasing the younger members of the population and also the availability of committed local help.

A 'supporters club', 150 strong, fundraises and helps with practical tasks. This club comprises people born or associated with Lövvik who now live elsewhere but want to retain the link. When questioned about whether Lövvik will still be going strong in 20 years' time, ex-teacher and local activist, Hervor Dahlén, speaks without hesitation: 'Of course, why not?'

Switzerland
Waltensburg has a population of 350 and sits 1,050 metres (3,445 feet) above the Upper Rhine Valley. This is a bilingual village where Swiss German and Surselvish are spoken. Remoteness, lack of resources, the persistent loss of young people and replacement by pensions, have all taken their toll.

In 1976 a property group backed by German capital proposed building 50 holiday chalets in Waltensburg. After long and heated debate the parish council – as planning authority – rejected this proposal. Instead a local co-operative was born called the 'Four-leafed Clover' (*Genossenschaft Quaterfegl*). By 1983 they had financed and built a £1.3 million 50-bedroom hotel, constructed in line with strict 'green tourism' principles. Bernard Lane, of Bristol University's Rural Tourism Unit, found that 'leaders of the initiative required considerable courage and stamina to press on with the scheme. Their resolve was strengthened by a steady flow of assistance from outside the area. Among the most important sources of both intellectual stimulation and technical help were the University and Technical High School in Zurich.'

So why is this significant? Desks, dressing tables and other furniture were constructed by carpenters on site – bought-in items were avoided so as to maximise the local labour input. Solar energy provides 27 per cent of the hotel's total energy requirement and wood for the heating system is harvested from forests owned by the Parish; this has brought dilapidated coppices back into productive use. Around 18 staff are employed full-time and another 13 are part-timers; 6 of the former and all the part-time workers come originally from Waltensburg. Occupancy averages 68 per cent through the year in contrast to the regional figure of 40 per cent. Bernard Lane concludes:

> there has been some disappointment that other Swiss rural communities have not copied the Waltensburg model. This is not entirely surprising. Switzerland has a great interest in its rural communities and in green issues but is a very conservative

society, not given to rushing into new, alternative activities. Hotel Ucliva has been successful because of the remarkable combination of skills, imagination, determination, contacts and courage possessed by the founding local group.

A crucial factor has been the sale of shares to those, throughout Switzerland, who are in sympathy with the project. Share capital funded the scheme and ensured future occupancy, because dividends come as discounts on room bookings. Without this form of funding and marketing the hotel would never have been built. Here is a stirring examaple of tenacity, combined with informed local leadership, matched by outside assistance.

In these European examples the detail is relatively unimportant, because culture, legal structures and geography will vary immensely. But the essential point is to sift and apply underlying principles to our own circumstances. Bengt Dahlgren celebrates the uniqueness of individual rural areas and argues that 'what is special about development in a local manner is that, in many ways, it goes against established procedures. It is the place that is important not the sector, the amateur not the expert, differences not similarities.' Charlie McConnell of the Community Development Foundation, a charity, advocates this type of active citizenship as a means of 'tackling the seemingly entrenched problems of underdeveloped, deprived and disadvantaged areas ... the development and regeneration of any community can take many forms, and is determined by the quality of the partnership and dialogue between government and people, and of course resources'.

Paradise Regained

Step 1

The first step towards 'Another Country' is set out by ECOVAST, which proposes 'a balance, and mutual support, between people and the environment. We look for integrated action between different arms of government, and between government and local people. We expect the local people to be consulted and involved.' Balance, integration and meaningful local participation are seen as keys to effective rural development. Encouragingly, both of the 'higher' tiers of local government in England have committed themselves to closer ties with parish and town councils. The Association of County Councils contends that 'larger authorities would have considerable scope and a direct interest in working with parish and town councils or developing area structures to provide very local services and representation'. Meanwhile the Association of District Councils 'supports the important and continuing role of parish councils, and in particular, their role in articulating and representing the views of village communities in rural areas'. This is an encouraging start, but the will must outlast any political posturing in the light of the current Local Government Review. The NALC, representing parish-level government, urges the 'devolution of activity in all appropriate cases from the principal authorities to those local councils willing and able to take on a wider role'. Bedfordshire and Dunstable have led the way on this and future arrangements will hinge upon the willingness of different authorities to agree terms and demonstrate their capability in managing varied responsibilities. The concept of 'subsidiarity' needs to be adopted at every institutional level from Brussels downwards.

Step 2

National and local government must, according to ECOVAST, 'recognise the special qualities of rural areas and needs of rural communities; and ... reflect these in integrated Rural Strategies and in all relevant sectoral policies'. Standardised programmes fail to reflect the variation in character of localities. Policies and programmes, brought to bear on an area, are like a foreign plant which, according to Michael Dower, 'can only flourish in a place if it is grafted onto a healthy local stock. You cannot expect a programme to take root just be "parachuting" it in: it has to "connect" with the way things are done in the area.' To bring real, lasting, benefit there must be a coherent link between EC, national and local activities.

Rural Voice (RV) calls for action

at a national and regional level to articulate goals, provide a clear framework of planning policies, and state broad programmes of investment. But it is at County, and then at District, level that the greatest opportunities exist to achieve the effective expression of goals, the pursuit of land use planning and the integrated implementation of investment programmes.

RV proposes that existing land use Development Plans prepared by the counties and districts, should be completed by a 'statement of goals for the future of the rural areas'. This would be prepared by the local authorities after widespread consultation within the area, which would take on board the findings of village appraisals. 'An integrated programme of public investment' and other means of intervention would also be pursued. This should be funded on the sort of co-operative basis inherent in the Peak Park IRD Programme, and would target the agreed goals for the area. In 1992 English Nature and the Countryside and Rural Development Commissions jointly supported

the preparation of comprehensive 'rural strategies' to take account of the relationship between economic, social, environmental and other factors . . . the extent to which a rural strategy engenders visible action 'on the ground', and change in rural communities, will provide a test of its success . . ., it should help build confidence amongst rural communities in the commitment of the partner organisations and their willingness to be flexible in pursuing the most appropriate action for the overall needs of a particular area.

On a parallel track, planners Ray Green and John Holliday have suggested that 'statutory countryside centres' could

be established at a strategic level in local authorities . . .. In practice these centres would be complementary to the development plan system but they would exert a country thrust against the urban thrust that currently prevails.

Effective integrated action in a particular geographic or topic area doesn't require anything as ambitious as the preparation of a Rural Development Strategy (RDS). But an RDS can, at best, help co-ordinate the direction and resources of many bodies influencing the countryside and, at least, increase contact between individuals, leading to an improved climate of co-operation.

Step 3
Allied to the above, if Integrated Rural Development along the lines of the Peak Park model is to be tried on a larger scale 'then ways must be found to loosen the rather rigid divisions between budgets set aside for different purposes and the administrative arrangements for controlling them. This applies to all levels of public administration right up to the European Commission . . . .'

The Peak Park Trust argues that limited term projects distract attention 'from the structure and content of the existing agencies. We are in favour of pilots and experiments, but they are of greatest potential use when their central objectives include a critical focus on established organisations, and not just the spaces in between.'

Step 4
Rural deprivation is a reality. The 1992 NCVO Survey of 'Rural Deprivation and Voluntary Organisations and Groups' points to a need for more time, money and volunteers with which to tackle disadvantage. A majority of respondents would welcome greater information and specialised training as a starting point. The reearchers argued that stable, well-resourced voluntary organisations were best placed to articulate and counter rural deprivation. Responses to it require professionals radically to rethink both their own role, and the potential input and status afforded to local non-professionals. Again, as the Peak Park Trust comments:

It is a deprivation to have less money than most, to be denied services available elsewhere to comparable groups, to lose people, networks and places of value, to feel politically and culturally 'shut out'. It is a further (preventable) deprivation to be left undeveloped, because one's talents, energies and commitments are not fully engaged by those who set the pace of rural life.

The Trust calls for a much more rigorous interpretation and implementation of 'community development', as opposed to simply 'locally-based', strategies. Community development is a double-edged weapon – whoever wields this must have a clear understanding of who it is intended to protect or free, and who it may well cut down.

Community development should be about

- *Collective action*
- around *issues*
- which are believed to be *important*
- and which *directly affect* people (and therefore motivate them).
- An *agenda* and process which remains the *property of local initiators*.
- The provision of appropriate *support* (not control) to deprived people.
- Pressure which may include *campaign and conflict* as much as consensus.

Peak Park Trust, 1991

In other words to be meaningful community work must not only affect those most in need but involve them.

This book has stressed the importance of rural areas as a national asset: the fate of village life is not just, therefore, of limited interest. Recognition that rural areas have significant needs and problems is the first step towards remedial action. Public, private and voluntary sector contributions should be sought to reflect the scale and nature of rural disadvantage. However, additional resources to bolster the activities of rural agencies and complement traditional voluntary action must also be matched by new forms of decision making.

It is time for the English countryside to be seen as an asset and not a millstone around the nation's neck: the land and the people are one.

Decently paid jobs, affordable homes and help for a significant number of 'disadvantaged' rural people are desperately needed.

The EC 'Leader' Programme is showing the way to genuine community-based rural development and closer to home, the Civic Trust has been successfully working in places such as north Devon to recreate a living and attractive environment.

It is time for countrypeople to speak out. A vocal and active population can be heard by outside bodies. Many of those involved in English village development projects relish the challenges facing them and are enjoying seizing the initiative. This very positive and powerful view of community service must be built on.

Without definite action rural problems may continue to be obscured. But with effort, decline can be stemmed and we may yet see 'Another Country'.

Useful Addresses

Rural Development Commission
11 Cowley Street
London SW1P 3NA
Tel: 071-276 6969
Fax: 071-276 6940
or
141 Castle Street
Salisbury, Wilts SP1 3TP
Tel: 0722-336255
Fax: 0722-332769

Central government agency concerned with the well-being of people who live and work in England's rural areas.

ACRE (Action with Communities in Rural England)
Somerford Court
Somerford Road
Cirencester, Glos GL7 1TW
Tel: 0285-653477
Fax: 0285-654537

England's rural communities charity and the Association of 38 County Rural Community Councils (RCCs). Speaks out for the urgent needs of rural people and promotes practical community-based action. Also acts as secretariat for Rural Voice, an alliance of rural agencies.

NCVO (National Council for Voluntary Organisations) Rural Team
Regent's Wharf
8 All Saints Street
London N1 9RL
Tel: 071-713 6161
Fax: 071-713 6300

Promotes rural voluntary action.

Calouste Gulbenkian Foundation (UK Branch)
98 Portland Place
London W1N 4ET
Tel: 071-636 5313

Research and funding addressing aspects of rural disadvantage.

ECOVAST (European Council for
the Village and Small Town)
c/o Federation Nationale pour
L'Habitat Rural
27 Rue de la Rochefoucauld
F-75009 Paris
France
or
UK Contact: c/o Michael Dower
Countryside Commission
Cheltenham, Glos GL50 3RA
Tel: 0242-521381
Fax: 0242-226027

Established 1984 to further the
well-being of country
communities and safeguard the
rural heritage throughout Europe.

National Association of Local
Councils
108 Great Russell Street
London WC1B 3LD
Tel: 071-637 1865
Fax: 071-436 7451

National Association of Volunteer
Bureaux
St Peter's College
College Road
Saltley, Birmingham B8 3TE
Tel: 021-327 0265
Fax: 021-327 3696

National Association of Councils
for Voluntary Service
Third Floor
Arundel Court
177 Arundel Street
Sheffield S1 2NU
Tel: 0742-786636
Fax: 0742-787004

Refer for full information on
many organisations to NCVO,
The Voluntary Agencies Directory,
13th edn, NCVO Publications,
1993.

Specific subject areas

Disabled People in Rural Areas

National Disability Information
Project
100 Park Village East
London NW1 3SR
Tel: 071-387 2171
Fax: 071-388 0914

Disability Alliance Educational
and Research Association
Universal House
88–94 Wentworth Street
London E7 7SA
Tel: 071-247 8776
Fax: 071-247 8765

RADAR (Royal Association for
Disability and Rehabilitation)
25 Mortimer Street
London W1N 8AB
Tel: 071-637 5400
Fax: 071-637 1827

Health and Community Care

Royal Agricultural Benevolent
Institution
27 West Way
Oxford OX2 0QH
Tel: 0865-724931
A charity fighting hardship in the
farming community.

The Samaritans
10 The Grove
Slough SL1 1QP
Tel: 0753-532713
Fax: 0753-819004
Volunteers who befriend people
feeling desperate, lonely or suicidal.

Family Welfare Association
501–505 Kingsland Road
London E8 4AU
Tel: 071-254 6251

Carers National Association
29 Chilworth Mews
London W2 3RG
Tel: 071-724 7776

National Community Health
Resource
57 Chalton Street
London NW1 1HU
Tel: 071-383 3841

Housing and Homelessness

Centrepoint Soho
5th Floor
140a Gloucester Mansions
Cambridge Circus
London WC2H 8HD
Tel: 071-379 3466

Help the Aged
St James's Walk
London EC1R 0BE
Tel: 071-253 0253
Fax: 071-895 1407

Joseph Rowntree Foundation
The Homestead
40 Water End
York YO3 6LP
Tel: 0904-629241
Fax: 0904-620072
Sponsors independent research into
housing, policy and community care
issues.

Rural Housing Trust
3rd Floor
Victoria Chambers
16–18 Strutton Ground
London SW1P 2HP
Tel: 071-233 3444

Scottish Child
40 Shandwick Place
Edinburgh EH2 5RT
Tel: 031-220 6502

Housing Associations Charitable
Trust
Yeoman House
168–172 Old Street
London EC1V 9BP
Tel: 071-336 7774
Fax: 071-336 7721

Shelter
88 Old Street
London EC1V 9HU
Tel: 071-253 0202
Fax: 071-608 3325

Mental Health

Good Practices in Mental Health
380–384 Harrow Road
London W9 2HU
Tel: 071-289 2034

MIND (National Association for
Mental Health)
22 Harley Street
London W1N 2ED
Tel: 071-637 0741
Fax: 071-323 0061

National Schizophrenia Fellowship
28 Castle Street
Kingston-upon-Thames
Surrey KT1 1SS
Tel: 081-547 3937

Race Issues

Black Environment Network
Regent's Wharf
8 All Saints Street
London N1 9RL
Tel: 071-713 6161

Centre for Research in Ethnic
Relations
University of Warwick
Coventry CV4 7AL
Tel: 0203-523523
Fax: 0203-524324

Commission for Racial Equality
Elliot House
10–12 Allington Street
London SW1E 5EH
Tel: 071-828 7022
Fax: 071-630 7605

SIA
High Holborn House
49/51 Bedford Row
London WC1V 6DJ
Tel: 071-430 0811

Women in Rural Areas

Kids' Clubs Network
279–281 Whitechapel Road
London E1 1BY
Tel: 071-247 3009
Fax: 071-247 4490

National Alliance of Women's
Organisations
279–281 Whitechapel Road
London E1 1BY
Tel: 071-247 7052
Fax: 071-247 4490

National Federation of Women's
Institutes
104 New Kings Road
London SW6 4LY
Tel: 071-371 9300
Fax: 071-736 3652

Refer also to NCVO, *The Women's
Directory*, NCVO Publications,
1991.

Young People

National Youth Agency
17–23 Albion Street
Leicester LE1 6GD
Tel: 0533 471200

National Federation of Young
Farmers' Clubs
YFC Centre
National Agricultural Centre
Stoneleigh, Kenilworth
Warwickshire CV8 2LG
Tel: 0203-696544
Fax: 0203-696684

National Council for Voluntary
Youth Services
Coborn House
3 Coborn Road
London E3 2DA
Tel: 071-980 6712

Lesbians and Gay Men

London Lesbian and Gay
Switchboard
BM Switchboard
London WC1N 3XX
Tel: 071-837 7324

National Friend
BM Friend
London WC1N 3XX
Information, advice and support to
lesbians, gay men and bisexuals.
Local groups likely to be listed in
telephone directories.

Stonewall Lobby Group
2 Greycoat Place
London SW1P 1SB
Tel: 071-222 9007
Lobbying to achieve equal rights for
lesbians and gay men in the UK.

Bibliography

ACRE, *Involving the Private Sector in Rural Housing*, 1990.

ACRE, *Tackling Deprivation in Rural Areas.* Report for the Calouste Gulbenkian Foundation, 1990.

ACRE, 'Nearly a third of all rural council houses sold', *Rural Digest*, No. 5, 5 March 1992.

ACRE, 'Peak Dale Youth Club/Motorcycle Club', *Rural Digest*, No. 19, 24 September, 1992.

ACRE/Rural Development Commission, *Rural Housing Supply*, 1991.

ACRE/Rural Development Commission, *Rural Social Housing – Supply and Trends*, 1992.

ACRE/Sussex Rural Community Council, *Who Cares?*, 1992.

Archbishops' Commission on Rural Areas, *Faith in the Countryside*, Churchman Press, 1990.

The Archers, BBC Radio 4, 6 September 1992.

Arkleton Trust, *Supporting and Animating Community-based Rural Development in Europe – Some Lessons for Scotland?*, 1990.

Association of County Councils, *Retained Fire-fighters Help Save Lives and Property.* Undated leaflet.

Association of District Councils, 'Minister launches countryside employment programme at ADC conference, News Release, 20 May 1992.

Association of District Councils, *Views on the Local Government Review*, 1992.

Audit Commission, *Value for Money in the Fire Service: Some Strategic Issues to be Resolved*, Occasional Paper No. 1, September 1986.

Bassetlaw MIND Befriending Scheme, Bassetlaw MIND, October 1989.

Bell, A. and Sigsworth, A. *The Small Rural Primary School*, The Falmer Press, 1987.

Benfield, G., *Rural Deprivation and Community Work*, Occasional Paper No. 12, School of Social Studies, University College Swansea, 1990.

Berliner, W., 'Small mercies', *Education Guardian*, 8 September 1992.

Brown, G. and Nixon, E., 'A future from the past: Fletchertown', in J.G. Derounian, ed., *The Village Strikes Back*, Northern Network of Rural Development Programmes, 1992.

Button, E., *Rural Housing for Youth*, Centrepoint Soho Charity, 1992.

Cable, A., '10 things on Len in black and white', *The Sun*, 14 September 1991.

Carlisle, A., *Hansard*, 26 June 1992.

Champion, T., 'Marching across England's green and pleasant land: the progress of counterurbanisation', Department of Geography, University of Newcastle upon Tyne, 1991.

Champion, T. and Watkins, C., *People in the Countryside*, Paul Chapman Publishing Ltd, 1991.

Civic Trust Regeneration Unit, *New Heart for Ilfracombe*, 1990.

Clancy, R., 'Rise in rural homeless is bigger than in towns', *The Times*, 24 September 1991.

Clark, D., *Good Neighbours*, Joseph Rowntree Foundation, 1991.

Clark, D., 'Affordable housing in rural areas', Address to Conference, Community Council of Northumberland, 2 June 1992.

Clark, D., 'Local needs and building use', *Rural Viewpoint*, No. 50, August 1992.

Clark, D., 'Reviewing local government', *Rural Viewpoint*, October 1992.

Clark, D., *Rural Development Strategies in England*, Rural Development Strategies Conference Paper, 20 November 1992.

Clark, D., *The Rural Vote*, Landmark Publications, 1992.

Committee for Rural Hampshire, *Annual Report 1991/2,* 1992.

Community Care, 'Out of town – out of sight', editorial, 22 November 1984.

Community Council for Hertfordshire, 'Pathways to affordable housing in rural Hertfordshire', 1992.

Community Council for Wiltshire, *Annual Report 1990–91,* 1991.

Community Council for Wiltshire, *The Facts,* leaflet, 1991.

Community Council for Wiltshire, 'Rural incomes', information sheet, 1992.

Community Council of Devon, 'Land bank opens the door', *Village Green Magazine,* June 1992.

Community Council of Northumberland, *High Forest Community Appraisal,* 1992.

Community Council of Shropshire, *Village Cluster Playscheme Project Report,* 1990.

Community Development Foundation/National Coalition for Neighbourhoods, *Taking Communities Seriously,* 1992.

Coopers & Lybrand, *Consent upon a Sure Foundation: the Future Structure of Local Government,* Association of County Councils, 1992.

Coster, G., 'Another Country', *Weekend Guardian,* 1–2 June 1991.

CountryFile, *Racism in the Countryside,* report by R. Segar, BBC1 Television, 30 August 1992.

Countryside Commission, *New Opportunities for the Countryside,* Report of the Countryside Policy Review Panel, 1987.

Countryside Commission, English Nature and Rural Development Commission, *Rural Strategies,* 1992.

Cripps, Sir J., *Christmas Coals to Community Care,* National Council for Voluntary Organisations, 1985.

Dahlgren, B., 'Some reflections on the periphery', paper to US–Swedish Seminar on Development in Marginal Areas, Karlstad, 22–26 May 1989.

Darley, G., Hall, P. and Lock, D., *Tomorrow's New Communities,* Joseph Rowntree Foundation/Town and Country Planning Association, 1991.

Deacon, B., *Poverty and Deprivation in the South-West: a Preliminary Survey,* Child Poverty Action Group, 1987.

Denman, J., Lane, B. and Scott, I., *Doing By Learning,* ACRE Rural Adult Education Project, 1989.

Department of the Environment, *Planning Policy Guidance (PPG3): Housing,* March 1992.

Department of the Environment, 'Tim Yeo announces successful schemes under Rural Housing Programme', news release, 9 March 1992.

Derbyshire Family Health Services Authority, *General Practitioner Services in Rural Derbyshire,* 1991.

Derounian, J., *Rural Development in Sweden,* Northumberland Rural Development Programme, 1990.

Derounian, J., *The Village Strikes Back,* Northern Network of Rural Development Programmes, 1992.

Derounian, J.G., 'Lifelines to the poor', *The Telegraph,* Weekend Section, 28 April 1990.

Derounian, J.G., 'They all run after the farmer's wife', *The Telegraph* Weekend Section, 13 October 1990.

Derounian, J.G., *Review of English Rural Development Programmes,* Unpublished MPhil Thesis. University of Newcastle upon Tyne, Department of Town and Country Planning, 1991.

Derwent Rural Counselling Service, *Counselling Country People,* 1991.

Development Commission, *Guidelines for Joint Rural Development Programmes,* 1984.

Devon Study Group on Deprivation, *Rural Deprivation in Devon,* 1990.

District Planning Officers' Society, *Affordable Housing,* 1992.

Dower, M., *Development in Rural Areas.* Town and Country Planning Association Annual Conference, November 1988.

Dower, M., *Problems in Application of EEC Policies for Rural Development,* CEPFAR European Seminar Paper, 26–29 May 1991.

Dudgeon, P., ed., Village Voices, quoting Mitford, M.R. Sidgwick

& Jackson Ltd, 1989.

Eadie, F., 'Stress and suicides in farming', *Rural Viewpoint,* No. 50, August 1992.

Ellwood, S., Nutley, S., Tricker, M. and Waterston, P., *Parish and Town Councils in England: A Survey, HMSO, 1992.*

Esslemont, E. and Harrington, J., *Swings and Roundabouts – The Highs and Lows of Life for Pre-School Children and Their Families in Rural Powys,* Save the Children, 1991.

European Community, *Draft Communication to the Member States Laying Down Guidelines for the Community Initiative 'Leader',* Directorate General for Agriculture, 1990.

European Council for the Village and Small Town, *A Strategy for Rural Europe,* 1991.

Fabes, R. and Knowles, C., *Working with Young People in Rural Areas,* Leicester Polytechnic Occasional Paper, 1991.

Ford, J. and Wilcox, S., *Reducing Mortgage Arrears and Possessions,* Joseph Rowntree Foundation, 1992.

Fox, C., *Rural Tourism – Development – The Ballyhoura Experience,* paper to International School of Rural Development, University College Galway, 6 July 1991.

Francis, D. and Henderson, P., *Working with Rural Communities,* MacMillan, 1992.

Gilbert, J., 'Someone cares', *Social Work Today,* 22 February 1990.

Gledhill, R., 'Resurrection of hope', *The Times,* Life and Times Supplement, 17 April 1992.

Green, R. and Holliday, J., Country planning: a time for action', *The Planner,* 1 November 1991 pp. 6–9.

Goldsmith, J.E., 'Issues facing rural women', *Rural Viewpoint,* No. 50, August 1992.

Griffiths, Sir R., *Community Care: An Agenda for Action,* HMSO, 1988.

Halliday, J., *Migration in Devon,* University of Exeter, Department of Geography, 1989.

Hampshire Council of Community Service, *Partnership in Rural Communities – Health and Community Care,* 1992.

Hampshire County Council, *Rural Initiative Report*, April 1990–April 1991, 1991.

Hampshire County Council/Committee for Rural Hampshire, *Hampshire Rural Development Strategy*, 1991.

Help the Aged, *Growing Old in the Countryside*, the CARE Project Housing Report, 1992.

Hexham Courant, 'Furniture scheme is helping the needy', 29 May 1992, p. 7.

Hill, B., Brookes, G. and Young, N., *Alternative Support Systems for Rural Areas, Volume 1*, Report for the Department of the Environment and MAFF, CEAS Consultants (Wye) Ltd, 1989.

Howkins, A., 'Peace of the country', *New Statesman and Society*, 4 August 1989.

HMSO, *English House Condition Survey*, 1988.

Housing Corporation, *Annual Report 1991/2*, 1992.

Hugh-Jones, S., 'Using the vital statistics', *Rural Viewpoint*, January 1988.

Info Rurale, 'Reporting on farmer Samaritans', June 1992.

Ivens, K., 'Racists all?', *The Telegraph*, letter to the editor, 29 April 1991.

Jaeger, H., *Rural Development Initiatives in England and Wales*, University of Reading Research Paper in Environmental Policy, 1989.

Jay, E., *Keep Them in Birmingham*, Commission for Racial Equality, 1992.

Joseph Rowntree Foundation, *Affordable Housing in Europe*, 1990.

Joseph Rowntree Foundation, *Involving the Private Sector in Rural Housing*, 1990.

Joseph Rowntree Foundation, *National Survey of Volunteering*, Social Policy Research Findings No. 22, December 1991.

Keane, M.J. and Quinn, J., *Rural Development and Rural Tourism*, Social Sciences Research Centre, University College Galway, 1990.

Kids' Clubs Network, *Report of Survey of Schools Out-of-School Care Provision*, 1990.

Laing, S., 'Images of the rural in popular culture 1950–1990', in

B. Short, ed., *The English Rural Community*, Cambridge University Press, 1992.

Lane, B., *The Hotel Ucliva Waltensburg/Vuorz, Switzerland,* University of Bristol, Department for Continuing Education, 1989.

Lees, A., 'Rural rights: rural charter', ACRE press release, July 1992.

The Listener, 22 May 1986, p. 20.

'Living on the streets', *The Guardian*, Education Section, 8 January 1991.

Lloyd, C., *Personal Accessibility and Isolation Survey,* Community Council of Lancashire, 1991.

Luff, G., 'Fire service estimates', *County Councils Gazette,* September 1990.

Lunn, T., 'Social work on wheels', *Community Care,* 13 October 1988.

McConnell, C., *Promoting Community Development in Europe,* Community Development Foundation, 1991.

Mackay, G. and Macleod, Y., *Rural Scotland Price Survey,* Report, Summer 1992.

McLaughlin, B.P., *Rural England in the 1980s, Rural Deprivation Study – Summary of Findings,* Essex Institute of Higher Education for the Development Commission/Department of the Environment, 1986.

MacSharry, R., 'Rural development – the challenge of the 1990's, Bass Irish Lecture, Belfast, 26 February 1990.

Major, J. Rt Hon., Speech to Oxford Farming Conference, 6 January 1992.

Mintel International Group, *Regional Lifestyles 1992,* 1992.

Moseley, M., 'Is rural deprivation really rural?', *The Planner,* July 1980.

Moseley, M., 'Lack of rural policy', *Rural Viewpoint,* No. 35, February 1990.

Moseley, M., 'Trends in rural areas', *Rural Viewpoint,* No. 46, December 1991.

National Alliance of Women's Organisations/Rural Development Commission/NCVO, *Women in Rural Areas – Challenges and*

Choices, 1992.

National Association of Local Councils, Response to Consultation Paper from DoE, 'The role of parish and town councils in England', First Draft, 1992.

National Children's Home, *Poverty and Nutrition Survey,* 1991.

NCVO, *Changing the Balance – Power and People Who Use Services,* 1991.

NCVO, *Equal Opportunities – A Starter Pack for Groups in Rural Areas,* Prepared by M.K. Stone, 1989.

NCVO, *Celebrating Women in Rural Voluntary Action,* 1991.

NCVO, *Out of Sight, Out of Mind, Out of Reach?,* 1992.

Nelson, S., 'Women who live in fear and rural isolation', *The Independent,* 23 March 1988.

Newby, H., *The Countryside in Question,* Hutchinson, 1988.

Norfolk Rural Community Council, *Helping Young People in Rural Norfolk,* 1991.

Norfolk Rural Community Council, *Parish Muscle: European Strength,* 1992.

North West Leicestershire Rural Child Care Scheme, *Background to the Rural Childcare Scheme,* 1992.

Northumberland County Council/Northern Region Low Pay Unit, *Low Pay in Northumberland,* 1991.

Northumberland County Council/Rural Development Programme, *Report of a Survey of Households Without Mains Services,* 1988.

Northumberland Health Authority, *Annual Report of the Director of Public Health,* 1991.

O'Cinneide, M. and Grimes, S., *Planning and Development of Marginal Areas,* Centre for Development Studies, University College Galway, 1992.

OECD, *Partnerships for Rural Development,* 1990.

OPCS, *General Household Survey,* HMSO, 1985.

OPCS, *General Household Survey, Preliminary Results,* 1990.

Orwin, C.S., *Forty Square Miles,* Ministry of Information, 1945.

Osmond, R., *Squaring the Circle,* Circle of Care, 1992.

Parker, K., Tricker, M. and Honey, J., *Two Villages, Two Valleys,*

The Peak District Integrated Rural Development Project 1981–88, Peak Park Joint Planning Board, 1990.

Pearson, D., 'The country coda', *ADC Review,* July 1991.

Philip, N., *Between Earth and Sky,* Penguin Books, 1984.

Phillips, D., 'Regarding rural young people', *Rural Viewpoint,* No. 47, February 1992.

Porter, D., *Hansard,* Adjournment Debate, 9 July 1992.

Priestley, J.B., *The Beauty of Britain,* B.T. Batsford Ltd, 1937.

Punters, Radio 4, 23 November 1988.

RASE/ADAS, *Stimulating the Rural Economy – New Approaches,* 1992.

Rendell, R. and Ward, C., quoting A. de Tocqueville, *Undermining the Central Line,* Chatto Counter Blast Number 7, 1989.

Renshaw, J. and Andrews, C., 'Mental health in the countryside', *Social Work Today,* 23 February 1989.

Roe, N., 'Silent plight', *County Living,* December 1990.

Royal Agricultural Benevolent Institution, *Fighting Hardship in the Farming Community,* 1991.

Royal Colleges of Physicians of the UK, *Housing or Homelessness: Public Health Perspective,* 1991.

Royal Town Planning Institute, *Planning Policy and Social Housing,* a discussion paper prepared by the Housing Panel, 1992.

Rural Development Commission, *English Village Services in the Eighties,* Research Series No. 7, 1990.

Rural Development Commission, *The Provision of Basic Utilities in Rural Areas,* prepared by Arup Economic Consultants, Research Series No. 6, 1990.

Rural Development Commission, *Corporate Plan 1992–95,* 1991.

Rural Development Commission, *Meeting the Challenge of Agricultural Adjustment,* 1991.

Rural Development Commission, *The Peace Dividend: A Preliminary Assessment of its Impact on Rural England,* 1991.

Rural Development Commission, 'Re-seeding the rural economy', *Rural Focus,* Vol. 5, No. 2, Summer 1991.

Rural Development Commission, *Rural Childcare,* Research Series

No. 9, written by M.K. Stone, 1991.

Rural Development Commission, *Women and Employment in Rural Areas,* Research Series No. 10, prepared by the Royal Agricultural Society of England, 1991.

Rural Development Commission, 'A living countryside – special issue', *Rural Focus,* Vol. 6, 1992.

Rural Development Commission, *Annual Report 1991/2,* 1992.

Rural Development Commission, *Homelessness in Rural Areas,* Research Series No. 12, 1992.

Rural Development Commission, *Summary and Findings – 1991 Survey of Rural Services,* 1992.

Rural Development Commission, *The Review of Priority Areas,* 1992.

'Rural front line troops need feedback on impact', *Planning,* No. 985, 11 September 1992.

Rural Voice, *A Rural Strategy,* 1987.

Rural Voice, *Planning as a Creative Force,* 1990.

Rural Voice Health Group, *Health Care in Rural England,* ACRE, 1992.

Russell, A., *The Country Parish,* SPCK, 1986.

Sarre, P., Phillips, D. and Skellington, R., *Ethnic Minority Housing: Explanations and Policies,* Aldershot, Gower, 1989.

Scott, D., Shenton, N. and Healey, B., *Hidden Deprivation in the Countryside,* Peak Park Trust, 1991.

Scottish Child, *Homeless Voices Report,* 1991.

Scottish Office, *Scottish Rural Life,* HMSO, 1992.

Shenton, N., Kirrage, G. and Scott, D., *Rural Deprivation and Voluntary Organisations/Groups,* National Council for Voluntary Organisations, 1992. In conjunction with the Community Council of Devon and Peak Park Trust.

Short, B., *The English Rural Community,* Cambridge University Press, 1992.

Shucksmith, M., *Rural Disadvantage,* Draft Report to COSLA, SDA, HIDB and Scottish Homes, University of Aberdeen, 1990.

Shuttleworth, Lord, *Hansard,* 26 June 1992.

South Lincolnshire Community Health Council, District Health Authority and Community Council of Lincolnshire, *The Provision of Health Care to Rural Populations: Grasping the Nettle*, 1991.

Soyinka, W., 'The telephone conversation', in F. Ademola, ed., *Reflections*, African Universities Press Ltd, 1962.

Standing Conference of RCCs, *Decline of Rural Services*, NCVO, 1978.

Stewart, J., 'Local government elsewhere in Europe', *Rural Viewpoint*, April 1992, p. 15.

Suffolk ACRE, Integration of Newcomers, 1990.

Suffolk Carers Support Project, *A Report and Evaluation, June 1988–October 1990*, 1991.

Sundon Village Appraisal Group, *Sundon Village – An Appraisal*, 1990.

Sussex Rural Community Council, 'Focus on Sussex's second wave of NHS trust applications', *Rural Health and Care Bulletin*, July 1991.

Sussex Rural Community Council, 'Campanology and castanets', *Sussex Rural News*, Autumn 1991.

The Post Office/ACRE, *Country Post. The Role of the Post Office in Rural Areas*, 1991.

The Times, 'Jobs plea for disabled', 3 August 1992.

The Times, 'Let repossessed homes to the homeless', 11 August 1992.

Transnational Team, 'Integrated Rural Action', *Results and Prospects – Rural Poverty and Deprivation in Europe*, Commission of the European Communities, 1989.

Transport and General Workers' Union, *Rural Areas*, Briefing Notes, 1991.

University of East Anglia Economics Research Centre, *US Military Expenditure in East Anglia*, 1989.

Uttley, A., *The Country Child*, Faber and Faber, 1945.

Vinson, Lord, 'More than green trees grow in the countryside', Rural Development Commission news release, 18 October 1989.

Volunteer Centre UK, *The Involvement of Volunteers in Rural Areas of England*, Research Paper No. 4, 1991.

Wallace, C., Dunkerley, D. and Cheal, B., 'Young people in rural Southwest England', in *Youth and Policy*, No. 33, 1991.

Wansbeck District Council, *Wansbeck District Local Plan, Introduction 1988–2000*, 1988.

Watt, J., 'Newcomers', *Counry Life*, 29 October 1992.

Westminster, Duke of, *The Problems in Rural Areas*, Business in the Community, 1992.

White, P., *Working with Rural Youth*, National Youth Agency, 1991.

Wibberley, G., *Countryside Planning – A Personal Evaluation*, Department of Environmental Studies and Countryside Planning, Wye College, Occasional Paper No. 7, 1982.

Wilkinson, J., 'Thursday's children', *Health Service Journal*, 2 April 1992.

Williams, R., *The Country and The City*, Paladin, 1975.

Williams, W.M., *The Country Craftsman*, Routledge and Kegan Paul, 1958.

Wilson, M., 'Teamwork backs a holistic approach to mental health', *Social Work Today*, 22 February 1990.

Women's Farm and Garden Association, *The Hidden Workforce*, 1989.

Woollett, S., *Counting the Rural Cost*, National Council for Voluntary Organisations, 1990.

World Health Organisation, European Region, *A Common Health Policy for All European Countries*, 1980.

Wye College, University of London, *Rural Society: Issues for the Nineties*, Papers given at the 11th Agricola Conference, 1991.

Young, C., *Caring For People – A Rural Perspective*, National Council for Voluntary Organisations, 1990.

Young, C., *Planning for Rural Care*, National Council for Voluntary Organisations, 1990.

Young, C., 'Caring for rural people', *Caring for People*, No. 7, Department of Health, 1991.

Young, K., 'Does the countryside matter?', *Countryside Commission News*, No. 34, November/December 1988.

Index